Mel Bay Presents

MW00827073

THE TOMÁS CRUZ CONGA METHOD

VOLUME II • INTERMEDIATE
Essential Cuban Conga Rhythms

by **Tomás Cruz**
with **Kevin Moore,**
Mike Gerald and Orlando Fiol

Cover Design: Bill Wolfer bill@mamborama.com
Recording studio photos: Tom Ehrlich tjejazz@sbcglobal.net
DVD Recorded at: Little Gypsy Studios, Santa Cruz, CA
Skin on Skin Congas provided by: Javier Muñiz

1 2 3 4 5 6 7 8 9 0

Visit us on the Web at www.melbay.com — E-mail us at email@melbay.com

Table of Contents

PART 4: MARCHAS FROM OLDER CUBAN POP MUSIC

PART 5: SONGO

PART 6: MARCHAS FROM NON-CUBAN RHYTHMS

PART 7: RECURSOS AND SOLOING

APPENDIX 1: MARCHAS NOTATED IN 8TH NOTES

APPENDIX 2: UNDERSTANDING CLAVE

APPENDIX 3: BOTA AND SONGO CON EFECTOS

Preface to the Tomás Cruz Conga Method Book/DVD Series

The Mystery of Modern Cuban Conga Playing

Most congueros, whether students or professionals, quickly find themselves on an emotional roller coaster when they first go to Cuba or to hear a modern Cuban band on tour. It begins with shock – the level of musicianship, even among 12 and 13 year old kids, is astounding. Shock gives way to euphoria as the newcomer realizes that he or she has just stumbled on perhaps the most creative chapter in the history of Latin music. Euphoria gives way to a determination to learn this new style, and finally, confusion and frustration reign supreme! Latin percussion usually involves learning a different set of fairly strict rhythmic patterns for each style, but what patterns are these Cubans using? The groove is overwhelming, but the conguero almost seems to be improvising. It's hard to pick out the pattern because it keeps changing, and the same problems come up when trying to analyze the patterns of the drums, timbales, bongó, bass and piano.

The next step, of course, is to seek help, but the vast majority of teachers and methods, both inside and outside of Cuba, begin by teaching basic historical rhythms and never seem to get to what's actually being played in today's Cuban concerts. And most videos and method books by famous virtuoso congueros tend to focus on soloing or pedagogic exercises rather than the actual content of the recordings and concerts which inspired the student's interest in the first place. The magical groove of the modern Cuban rhythm section remains a mystery.

Solving the Mystery – The Story of the Tomás Cruz Conga Method

We were determined not to let these books fall into the same traps as their predecessors, so to ensure we'd get to the final goal, we started at the end and worked backwards. We tackled Volume III first, immersing ourselves in the real music that's being played in the nightclubs and concert halls of Havana today – the music of the leading bands of Cuba – Paulito FG, Manolín (El Médico de la Salsa), Los Van Van, NG La Banda, Bamboleo, Klimax, Issac Delgado, Manolito y su Trabuco, Charanga Habanera, Carlos Manuel, Azúcar Negra, etc. As anyone who's heard these bands live will testify, you can study Mambo, Guaracha and Salsa for a lifetime and still have no idea whatsoever what the congueros are doing in this type of music!

So our first step was to find one of the leading congueros of the modern Cuban style and we were lucky enough to discover that our dream candidate had recently moved to Miami and was willing to take on the project. Tomás "Tomasito" Cruz grew up in the middle of the musical revolution that took place in Havana in the 90's. It was he who invented and performed the ground-breaking conga parts on perhaps the greatest Timba album ever recorded, Paulito FG's "Con la conciencia tranquila". After relocating to Miami in 1998, he joined another of the leading Timba bands, "Manolín, El Médico de la Salsa". He also plays with top traditional Latin artists such as Celia Cruz and Willie Chirino.

The second step was to cut through the verbiage and ask Tomás to demonstrate *exactly* what he plays, all the way through, on specific songs from Paulito FG's legendary "Con la conciencia tranquila" and various Timba classics from Tomasito's current group, "El Médico de la Salsa". We videotaped him playing along with his own recordings and then asked him to study the video footage, explain his approach, analyze the arrangement as a whole, and isolate key patterns and techniques. For each rhythm taught in Volume III, we tell you exactly where to find it on a specific recording. These are not "etudes" or exercises invented for the sake of writing a method book – this is the real deal.

The next task was to present the rhythms in such a simple way that readers would be able to learn them quickly and without frustration – not just watch the DVD once and then file it away with the other method books for future reference. We created a simple and clear notation system which combines standard rhythmic notation with easy to understand letters which can be easily read by those who don't read music, and then we went a step further by inventing the **Step by Step DVD Method**, which makes it fast and easy to learn the patterns without even looking at the book. An equally important advantage of the DVD method is that, instead of spending time trying to decipher printed notation, all of the student's practice time is spent in rhythm, watching one of the world's funkiest congueros and absorbing the intangible nuances of his technique and body language.

Satisfied that Volume III had accomplished its goal, we began Volume II, which covers the roots of Timba – the Cuban, Afro-Cuban and non-Cuban rhythms invented prior to 1990 which formed the rhythmic vocabulary of the Timba pioneers – rhythms such as Songo, Mozambique, Bomba, Guaguancó, 6/8, etc. Volume II also uses the Step by Step DVD Method, but the rhythms are considerably easier. Like Volume III, Volume II gives you the music history to go with the patterns and identifies classic recordings on which they can be found.

Finally, we wrote Volume I, in which Tomasito reveals the time-tested conga method which he himself studied with Changuito and other master congueros at the ENA conservatory in Havana. Volume I starts at the absolute beginning and is designed for the person who has never touched the congas, but is also of great value to the advanced player who wishes to understand the foundation and rudiments of the approach that has allowed the ENA and the other Havana conservatories to consistently turn out so many world-class congueros each year. Volume I begins with simple exercises to develop technique and systematically works its way to basic rhythm patterns such as Salsa, Chachachá and Bolero, which are presented using the Step by Step DVD method. It also contains an extensive series of rudiments and "recursos" for use in solos and fills. This is continued in Volume II.

The Tomás Cruz Conga Method
Volume I - Beginning
Conga Technique as Taught in Cuba
Mel Bay Catalog #20299DP

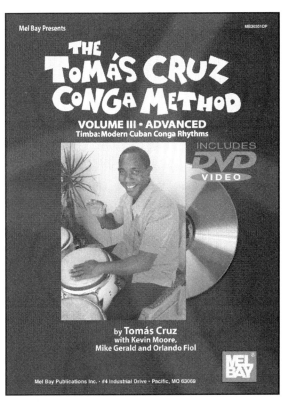

The Tomás Cruz Conga Method
Volume III - Advanced
Timba: Modern Cuban Conga Rhythms
Mel Bay Catalog #20301DP

ACKNOWLEDGEMENTS

Tomás Cruz: Este libro es el resultado de mucho estudio, sacrificio y dedicación, el mismo no se pudiera haber escrito sin la ayuda de muchas personas, a las cuales quiero darles mi agradecimiento.

Tuve mis primeros estudios en la E.V.A. (Escuela Vocacional de Arte) en Pinar del Río, Cuba, donde mis maestros fueron muy estrictos y grandiosos (Gilberto, Tomas Torre, Néstor Luis y Héctor). También quiero agradecer a mis maestros de solfeo, historia de la música, piano, etc.

A mis grandes amigos y compañeros de estudios de mi año (Omar Rojas, Ciro Parlá, Eddie Pérez, Jorge Castillo, Iván González, Iliana Castillo, Ademilis Hernández) que fueron consejeros y compañía en mi vida.

Vale reconocer la presencia de una persona, a la cual yo quiero y admiro mucho: José Luis Quintana (Changuito) por haberme enseñado la belleza, la técnica y la magia de la Conga. Junto a mí, otros estudiantes como Yoel del Sol, Carlos Reyes, Pedro Pablo Martínez, que tuvieron la suerte de haber aprendido este estilo maravilloso.

También quiero mencionar a una persona muy especial en mi vida (Adolfo Orta, mi maestro de trombón, que mas bien no fue maestro, fue un amigo).

Quiero darle las gracias a mi maestro de Batá, Nardo (el Gollo) que me dió la posibilidad de aprender un instrumento tan lindo y rico en ritmo, el cual me ayudó y me dio capacidad en mi mente para mezclar y combinar ritmo de Batá con la Conga.

Es muy importante señalar mis compañeros de banda, Yoel Páez, Yoel Domínguez, Sergio Noroña, Fran Rubio, Yosvel Bernal, Alexander Abreu, Joaquín Díaz, Carlos Pérez, Juan Manuel Ceruto, por haberme ayudado a enriquecer mi mente de su sabiduría.

Quiero hablar sobre la persona más importante en el proceso de este libro, una persona de una inteligencia genial, a la cual le doy las gracias por ser el creador de la idea para hacer este libro: Kevin Moore. Además, agradecer a Mike Gerald por haber dedicado parte de su tiempo para escribir muy rápidamente este método de percusión, y gracias a Orlando Fiol por habernos aconsejado y ayudado con su gran experiencia en la cración de este libro.

Me gustaría mencionar en este agradecimiento los congueros, que fueron mis patrones a seguir: Jorge Alfonso (El Niño) y Angá (Irakere), Andrés Miranda (Negrón), Tomás Ramos, Juan Nogueras (Wickly), Tata Güines, los Papines, el Goyo (maestro del I.S.A.), José Luis Quintana (Changuito), Manolo (Van Van), Yulo (N.G. La Banda), Yoel Drigs, etc.

También quiero darle las gracias a timba.com, Duniel Deya, y a mi gente de California que me ayudaron en mi estancia allá: Michel, Johann, Alexis, Alain, Fito, Bárbara, Javier, Osvaldo, y Joanna.

Espero que este diferente y nuevo método ayude a todos los congueros a desarrollar la técnica de Timba de una manera rápida y eficaz para que el mundo cuente con buenos congueros.

English translation by Tanja Cruz: This book is the result of many years of studies, sacrifice and dedication and could not have been written without the support of many individuals, whom I would like to acknowledge.

My first studies took place at the E.V.A. Vocational School of Arts (Escuela Vocacional de Arte) in Pinar del Río, Cuba, where I had very strict and magnificent teachers (Gilberto, Tomás Torre, Néstor Luis and Héctor). Among others, I would like to thank my professors of solfeggio, music history and piano.

To my great friends and fellow students of my graduating class (Omar Rojas, Ciro Parlá, Eddie Pérez, Jorge Castillo, Iván González, Iliana Castillo, Ademilis Hernández) who gave me advice and were companions in my life.

I'd also like to acknowledge the presence of a person whom I greatly respect and admire: José Luis Quintana (Changuito) for teaching me the beauty, technique and magic of the Conga. Along with me, other students like Yoel del Sol, Carlos Reyes, Pedro Pablo Martínez had the opportunity to learn this marvelous style.

I would like to mention another special person in my life, Adolfo Orta, my trombone teacher, who was not just my teacher but my friend as well.

I want to express my gratitude to my teacher of Batá, Nardo (el Goyo) who gave me the opportunity to learn an instrument so beautiful and rich in rhythm, who helped me and allowed me to combine the rhythms of Batá with the Conga.

It's very important to acknowledge the musicians with whom I played and recorded: Yoel Páez, Yoel Domínguez, Sergio Noroña, Frank Rubio, Yosvel Bernal, Alexander Abreu, Joaquín Díaz, Carlos Pérez, Juan Manuel Ceruto, for helping me enrich my mind with their knowledge.

I would like to talk about the most important person in the process of creating this book, a person of great intelligence, whom I thank for creating the idea to make this book: Kevin Moore. Also, to thank Mike Gerald for having dedicated some of his time to write with great speed this method of percussion and Orlando Fiol for having given us the benefit of his great experience in the creation of these books.

In this acknowledgment, I'd also like to mention the conga players who were my models to follow: Jorge Alfonso (El Niño) and Angá (Irakere), Andrés Miranda (Negrón), Tomás Ramos, Juan Nogueras (Wickly), Tata Güines, los Papines, el Goyo (teacher at I.S.A.), José Luis Quintana (Changuito), Manolo (Los Van Van), El Yulo (NG La Banda), Yoel Drigs, etc.

I would also like to express my gratitude to timba.com, Duniel Deya, and to my friends in California who helped me during my stay over there: Michel, Johann, Alexey Berlind, Alain, Fito, Bárbara Valladares, Javier, Osvaldo, and Joanna Goldberg.

I hope that this new and different method will help all conga players develop their Timba technique in a fast and efficient way, so that the world will soon see more good conga players.

Kevin Moore, Mike Gerald & Orlando Fiol wish to thank:

<u>Conceptual Guidance:</u> David Peñalosa, Alexey Berlind, and Pepe Martínez.
<u>Production:</u> Neal Hellman, Sarah Belden, Jon Hansen, Doug Witherspoon, Ed Riegler, Christy Meyer, Bill Bay, Trevor Salloum, and above all, our graphics gurus, Bill Wolfer and Mig Gianino.
<u>Photography:</u> Tom Ehrlich (additional photos by Kevin Moore, Duniel Deya and Yoel Páez)
<u>Moral and Technical Support:</u> Wendy Black, Kathryn Van Eenoo, Tanja Cruz, Jorge Ginorio, Juan Tomás García, Javier Muñiz, Mike Lazarus, José Reyes, Mike Doran, María Carlota Domandi, Luis Carranza, Matthew Dubuque, Joanna Goldberg, Elena Peña & Nikki, Bruce Ishikawa, Majela Serrano, Hugo Cancio, Arnaldo Vargas, Steve Cervantes, Francisco Andrade, Edwin Morales, Bosco Gitano, Nina "La Reina del Merengue" Gómez, Mike Croy, Curtis Lanoue.
<u>Inspiration:</u> Rebeca Mauleón-Santana, Alberto Centelles, Juan Ceruto, Edduar Bernal, Yosvel Bernal, Yoel Páez, Yoel Domínguez, Giraldo Piloto, Calixto Oviedo, Reinier Guerra, Yulién Oviedo, Michael Spiro, Marty Sheller, Andrés Cuayo, Sergio Noroña, Carlos Caro, and above all, Tomás Cruz for his patience, perseverance and incredible insights into the secrets of music.

All recording session photography by Tom Ehrlich.

PART 1: INTRODUCTION

Introduction to the Series: The Tomás Cruz Conga Method

What?

The Tomás Cruz Conga Method is designed to quickly and comprehensively teach anyone, from a rank beginner to a professional conguero, to play congas as they're played in Cuba today. It can be studied using only the books, only the DVD's (Digital Video Disc), or a combination of the two.

Who?

Tomás "Tomasito" Cruz was born and raised in Cuba in the middle of the musical revolution of the 90's. By the time he relocated to Miami he had become one of the top congueros in Cuba, playing in what most Cuban music experts consider one of the two or three best Timba bands ever assembled, the 1997-98 incarnation of Paulito FG y su Élite which recorded the groundbreaking CD, "Con la conciencia tranquila". The creativity and drive of Tomasito's conga tumbaos on that album put him in the very upper echelon of the most competitive Latin music scene in the world. Similarly, it took

Tomasito very little time to rise to the top of the Miami Latin music scene, playing with Manolín, el Médico de la Salsa, Willie Chirino, Celia Cruz, and many others. He also has a thorough mastery of bongó, Batá, and a deep understanding of Cuban music as a whole. In short, when we set out to write a book explaining the mysteries of Cuban conga playing, Tomasito was our first choice by a considerable margin.

Why?

For many years it was extremely difficult to find recordings of modern Cuban music, much less to hear the bands live, but in the late 90's groups like Los Van Van and Paulito FG y su Élite began to tour the US, Europe and Japan, and Latin music fans and musicians alike were amazed when they heard the exciting new "Timba" style they were playing. Every instrument of the rhythm section had taken a quantum leap in terms of complexity and creative freedom. However, many of those who tried to learn this new approach found it significantly more difficult to understand than the Salsa commonly played outside of Cuba.

Problem #1: What exactly are they playing? Even those who have taken study courses in Cuba, which invariably seem limited to the fundamentals and history of traditional Cuban music, have found themselves just as dumbfounded upon hearing the modern groups in performance. In addition to the language and cultural barriers, the music is too new for the players themselves to have fully analyzed it...they're too busy *playing* it and adding to it to take time to dissect it and explain it. The albums themselves have so much going on that even professional musicians have difficulty transcribing individual parts by ear and the Timba style is so ambidextrous that even knowing whether to slap with the left or right hand becomes part of the jigsaw puzzle.

Solution: All of the patterns in Volume III are from real Timba albums, clearly notated, and spoon-fed to the reader stroke by stroke by means of a simple DVD method.

Problem #2: Where did all of these new ideas come from? The musicians cite the influences of Songo, Batá music, Rumba, Guaguancó, and even American funk and R&B, but what are these rhythms and how are they incorporated into Timba?

Solution: Volume II uses the same innovative teaching techniques to teach the rhythms and offers insights and listening recommendations to help the student grasp their significance.

Problem #3: How do they make it look so easy? These young musicians play with such fire and grace that trying to emulate them can be discouraging. How, without having been born and raised in Havana, can musicians get a little piece of that magic into their own playing?

Solution: Volume I spells out the method used to teach congas in the Cuban conservatories and the hours of DVD footage included in this course provide the opportunity to learn the feel of Cuban drumming by osmosis; to watch and play along with a master conguero as he breaks each pattern down note by note, with a steady rhythm groove playing throughout the exercise.

How?

At the heart of the Tomás Cruz Conga Method is a simple and effective DVD technique based on learning by imitation. Once you understand the simple process explained below, it's actually quite possible to learn each pattern with only the DVD, without reading music at all.

Tomasito plays the pattern at full speed, and then, in slow motion, accompanied by a special click track, he plays only the first stroke of the pattern and then waits for the beginning of the pattern to come around again. He repeats just the first stroke a total of 4 times. This gives the student 4 chances to learn and practice the hand movement, allowing Tomasito's tone, posture, time feel and technique to be assimilated "by osmosis", as he himself assimilated it by watching the greatest congueros of earlier generations during his childhood and adolescence in Cuba.

Tomás then adds the second stroke and repeats *this* cycle 4 times; then the third, and so on until the pattern is complete. It's extremely easy to keep up with the flow of the DVD because only a single stroke is added every four repetitions, and since each DVD chapter can be started over without the tedious rewinding necessary with a video tape, it's easy to go back to the beginning if you lose your place in the pattern. Thanks to the huge capacity of DVD discs, we were able to film Tomasito patiently building many of the patterns in this way. From the very beginning the student is playing in rhythm, and in clave, asked to learn only a single stroke at a time, and given the chance to master it before each additional stroke is added. Patterns that are too long to be appropriate for this method are demonstrated at full speed and in slow motion.

About the Coauthors

Kevin Moore is the music editor of the world's largest Cuban music website, www.timba.com, and the musical director of the American salsa band Orquesta Gitano (www.picadillo.com/gitano). He has studied with dozens of leading Cuban musicians, written many extensive articles on Cuban music, and served as a consultant for features and articles produced by the BBC, the Los Angeles Times, and musicologists from Harvard and other major universities.

Michael Gerald is a Canadian drummer who has spent 7 years studying and playing Timba and has recorded two albums with his group, Sol y Soul (solysoul.timba.com), which, aside from himself, is composed entirely of all-stars from the various Cuban supergroups.

Orlando Fiol, a professional pianist/conguero/composer in the Philadelphia area, began his studies of Latin music as a small child under the tutelage of his father, Latin recording artist Henry Fiol. In 1996 he traveled to Cuba where he studied and played with Pancho Quinto, Changuito, members of Sierra Maestra, Raíces Profundas and the Sexteto Habanero. He is also an expert in the fields of Jazz, classical music and Indian music, having been awarded a fellowship to study tabla and pakhawaj in India. Orlando's encyclopedic knowledge of the history of folkloric and Latin music, and his ability to communicate with Tomasito in fluent Spanish have proved indispensable in the writing of this series.

What is Timba?

Timba is the commonly accepted term for the new type of concert and dance music that's been played in Cuba since about 1989. While he plays all forms of Latin and Afro-Cuban folkloric music, Tomás Cruz is best know for his work with Timba groups, and it was this work that inspired the creation of this series.

Until the late 90's, it was impossible to hear live Timba without going to Cuba, and nearly as hard to acquire Timba recordings. To further complicate matters, music produced in Cuba was and still is, to a great degree, "blacklisted" in the United States and nearly never played on commercial radio. In spite of all these obstacles, Timba groups have been touring the United States and Europe regularly for the last 6 years and have inspired a rapidly growing, almost fanatic following, including American musicians such as coauthors Kevin Moore, Michael Gerald and Orlando Fiol.

The musical genre most closely related to Timba is Salsa, but Timba also contains strong influences from Afro-Cuban folkloric music, American R&B, Jazz, and various other forms of world pop music. A huge emphasis is placed on originality — not only in songwriting and arranging, but in the individual patterns played by each member of the rhythm section, and while this has resulted in a large number of classic recordings, it's also led to a great deal of frustration among musicians trying to learn to play Timba because the rhythm patterns are sometimes unique to each song. Helping people understand this wide range of rhythmic diversity is the primary goal of this series of books.

To learn more about Timba we recommend the website www.timba.com, which contains well over 100,000 words of articles and interviews edited by coauthor Kevin Moore (kevin@timba.com). There are also extensive audio examples and educational materials.

Who are the Leading Timba Bands?

There are about a dozen major Timba groups, with new ones springing up from time to time, and frequent shifting of key players from one band to another. The musical scene in Havana is so strong and closely-knit that each band seems to feed off the creativity of the others.

The most important groups, in approximate order of their appearance on the Timba scene, are Los Van Van, NG La Banda, Charanga Habanera, Issac Delgado, Paulito FG, El Médico de la Salsa, Klimax, Bamboleo, Manolito y su Trabuco, Azúcar Negra, Los Que Son Son, and Tirso Duarte.

Tomás Cruz played with Paulito FG and currently plays with El Médico de la Salsa (also known as Manolín). He played congas on four of the most important albums of the Timba genre:

Paulito FG: "Con la conciencia tranquila" (Nueva Fania NF-108)
Juan Ceruto: "Gracias Formell" (Ciocan Records HMC-2607)
Paulito FG: "El bueno soy yo" (also released as "Paulito FG") (Nueva Fania NF-104)
Manolín, El Médico de la Salsa: "El puente" (Ciocan Records HMC-2605)

Who are the other leading Timba congueros?

There are literally hundreds of phenomenal congueros in Cuba. Here's an incomplete list of some of the leading Timba congueros who tour outside of Cuba frequently. Each has his own page on www.timba.com, as does Tomasito (http://tomasito.timba.com).

Denis "Papacho" Savón
Issac Delgado Group
http://papacho.timba.com

Jorge Luis "Papiosco" Torres
founding member of Klimax
now tours with Cubanismo
http://papiosco.timba.com

Tomás "El Panga" Ramos
Tomasito's predecessor in
Paulito FG y su Élite
http://panga.timba.com

Duñesky Barreto
Bamboleo
http://dunesky.timba.com

Alexis "Mipa" Cuesta
Tomasito's predecessor with
El Médico de la Salsa
http://mipa.timba.com

Orlando Mengual
Charanga Habanera
http://orlandito.timba.com

Jorge "El Toro" Castillo
Los Que Son Son
http://eltoro.timba.com

Evelio Ramos
Manolito y su Trabuco
http://evelio.timba.com

Manuel "Manolo" Labarrera
Los Van Van
http://manolo.timba.com

Luis Guillermo Palacio
Carlos Manuel y su Clan; Sol y Soul

Yoel Cuesta
Azúcar Negra
(now with Adalberto Alvarez)
http://yoelcuesta.timba.com

Adel González
Irakere

Wickly Nogueras
original conguero of NG La Banda
http://wickly.timba.com

Tomás with Duñesky Barreto of Bamboleo
photos by Duniel Deya

Introduction to Volume II

Volume II is aimed at two distinct categories of readers:

1) Intermediate players who have completed Volume I and are ready for a wider range of rhythms to study and use in live playing situations.

2) Experienced congueros who have digested Volume III and now seek to understand the roots of the modern Cuban conga style.

Having assimilated the material in Volume I, the student should be able to play basic *son montuno, salsa, chachachá,* and *bolero.* But Latin music had to evolve for decades before the musical revolution of the 1990's that inspired this series of books became possible. Volume II, in fact, begins *centuries* before the *chachachá* and *bolero,* with the complex Afro-Cuban folkloric rhythms brought to Cuba and further developed by transplanted African slaves.

Next we explore a variety of secular dance rhythms such as *Pilón* and *Mozambique* from the isolated "Cold War" period between the "Ricky Ricardo" days and the fall of the Berlin Wall, during which time Cuban music evolved in a relative vacuum, while the internal and external politico-economic forces that contributed to the Timba movement reached the boiling point.

Next, we proceed to Timba's most direct predecessor – *Songo* – the genre name given to the vast and eclectic body of work produced between 1969 and 1990 by the most influential and successful group in the history of Cuba, *Los Van Van,* and its followers. In this extensive section we explore the breakthrough musical concepts of Los Van Van's three musical and rhythmic pioneers: Juan Formell, Pupy Pedroso, and Tomasito's teacher, José Luis "Changuito" Quintana.

Next, we diverge from our Cuba-centric point of view and explore the rhythms of three other important Latin countries: Puerto Rico, Colombia, and the Dominican Republic.

Finally, we resume the study of *recursos* and soloing which began in Volume I and discuss some of great conga soloists of the last 60 years.

The goal of Volume II is not to be an encyclopedia of rhythms. Volumes I & II are "prequels" which lead inevitably to Volume III, and share its ultimate focus – the heretofore undocumented breakthoughs in conga-playing that have occurred in Cuba since 1990. Thus, the marchas are not selected for completeness, or to be the most "generic" examples of each genre. They were selected by simply asking Tomasito which marchas he and his fellow Cuban congueros were familiar with before they found themselves at the epicenter of the brave new world of the 90's – those marchas most influential in developing their new approaches to playing the congas.

That said, Volume II also serves as a broad introduction to the vast world of pre-1990 conga music. An article and listening recommendations accompany each section, designed to help the reader acquire a taste for each genre and a feel for how it fits into the "big picture" of Latin music.

PART 2: HOW TO USE THIS BOOK

Notation

First of all, remember that it's quite possible to learn many of these patterns without ever looking at the notation. Our Step by Step DVD training Method allows you to learn them interactively by watching Tomasito and copying his hand movements. But we've also tried to devise the clearest possible method of notation, and added letters so that even a person who doesn't read music at all will be able to decipher the sequence of hand movements.

For example:

As you can see, even if you don't read music, and/or haven't learned the note shapes, you can learn the pattern by looking at the letters. The first row starts out with S B T S, which stands for **S**lap, **B**ass, **T**ip, **S**lap. The second row starts out with R L L R, which stands for **R**ight, **L**eft, **L**eft, **R**ight. When, as in the case of the 11th note, both hands play at the same time, one hand is written above and the other below. Alternatively, we sometimes write "S/O" instead of placing the second note above. Volume I teaches each of these strokes in detail.

Some of Tomasito's recordings use two congas and others use three. The high drum is written on the top space ("E"), the middle drum on the middle line ("B"), and the low drum on the bottom space ("F").

Open tones are notated with a round, solid notehead. The *tumba* (low) and *tres dos* (middle) drums are almost always played open. The quinto and tumba are also called the *macho* and *hembra* respectively. "Quinto" can also refer to the higher pitched solo drum in Rumba.

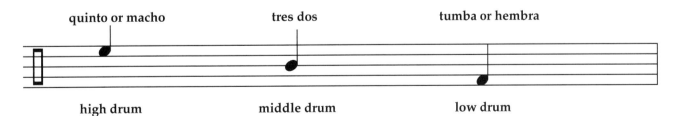

17

The high drum also uses up to seven other strokes, which are described and demonstrated in great detail in Volume 1:

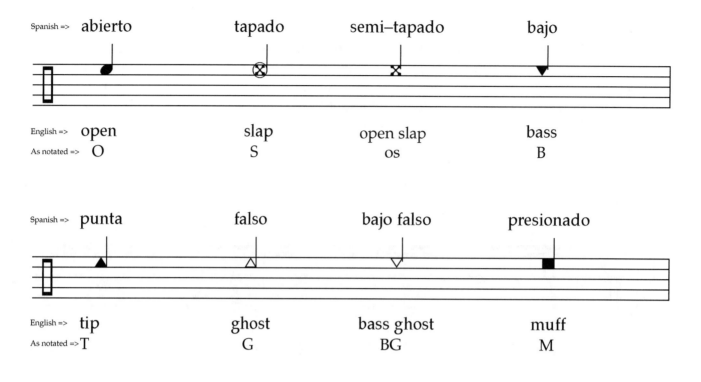

Spanish => **abierto**   **tapado**   **semi–tapado**   **bajo**

English => open   slap   open slap   bass
As notated => O   S   os   B

Spanish => **punta**   falso   bajo falso   presionado

English => tip   ghost   bass ghost   muff
As notated => T   G   BG   M

16^{ths} versus 8^{ths}

There's a lot of controversy over whether Cuban rhythms should be written in 8th or 16th notes. Writing in 16th notes is more common in Cuba while most American and European groups write their music in 8th notes. Each method has its advantages.

In terms of describing what's really taking place in the music there's no doubt that the 16th note approach is correct. All professional Latin musicians, regardless of how they notate it, *feel* the music such that there are only 4 beats per clave but writing it in 8th notes implies that there are eight. Trying to hear the beat twice as fast as it really is causes severe conceptual problems for students. Experienced musicians learn to look at 8th notes and play them in "cut time" so that they're feeling the beat correctly, but taking advantage of the fact that the 8th note notation is less cluttered with extra flags and beams and therefore easier on the eyes.

We have no desire to inconvenience experienced musicians who are already used to reading in 8^{ths}, so in each book we provide appendices with all of the marchas written in 8^{ths}.

How to Use the Step-by-Step DVD Training Method

At the heart of the Tomás Cruz Conga Method is a simple and effective new method of learning marchas by playing along with the enclosed DVD video. There's not enough room on the DVD to use this method for every marcha so Tomás has chosen the most appropriate candidates. For each marcha, there are two DVD chapters. The first is always played at full speed and the second is either played in slow motion, or taught using the Step-by-Step DVD Method.

For a tutorial on how the Step-by-Step DVD Method works, take a look at the marcha shown at the top of the next page, the *Guaguancó*:

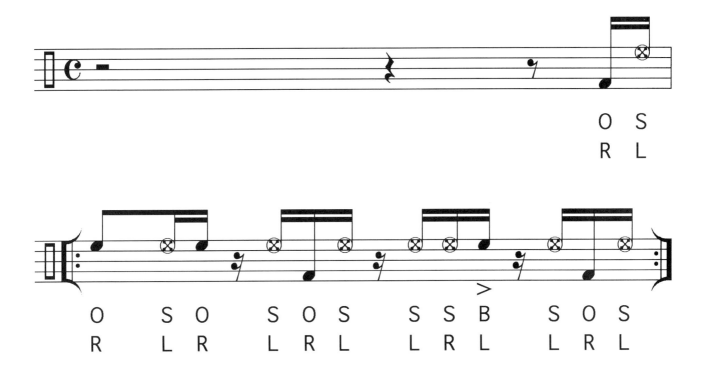

In DVD Chapter 1, Tomasito plays the marcha at full speed. Listen to this a few times until the marcha pattern becomes familiar. Singing along with the full speed DVD chapter is also an excellent idea. Make sure you hear and understand where the clave click track is before proceeding! If the clave confuses you, refer to Appendix 2, which explains this important concept in great detail.

Now go to DVD Chapter 2. This time the tempo is much slower. Again, listen carefully to the clave click track and clap along to again make sure you're hearing the clave correctly. Once the clave feels right, you're ready to start the exercise. Set up your congas so you can sit comfortably in front of your television set. Tomasito begins by playing just the first note of the pattern, then waits for the clave to run its course, and then repeats this cycle for a total of four times. As you watch the DVD, play along. It will be very easy because only one note is added at a time and you're given four chances to practice it before the next one is added. To warn you in advance what the next stroke will be there's also a vocal cue exactly 2 beats, or half a clave, before the beginning of the measure that contains the new stroke.

Every 4 claves, another stroke is added. You may not make it all the way through the exercise the first time, but thanks to the miracle of DVD, you need only press a button to return to the beginning, or to review DVD Chapter 1 to get the sound of the full speed marcha back into your ear. At the first sign of frustration, just start over. Learning complex marchas doesn't have to be hard if you only add one new note at a time. The whole idea of this exercise is that it's supposed to be easy. As soon as you feel yourself "trying", grab that remote control and start the exercise over. Remember that what you're learning subconsciously from staring at Tomasito's hands is *more* important than learning the pattern itself – it's the nuances of rhythm, tone and feeling that make his recordings and performances so satisfying and by practicing along with the DVD each day you'll begin to absorb these qualities into your own playing. The feeling of "swing" is difficult or impossible to explain in words, and there's no doubt that the best, if not the *only* way to learn it is the way Tomás himself learned it – by "osmosis". In Cuba, these subtleties are handed down from generation to generation by example – not by explanation – and you can use the DVD to let Tomasito hand a little of his magic down to you.

PART 3: AFRO-CUBAN FOLKLORIC MARCHAS

History does not always move in a straight line. It took centuries for modern Western science to return to the level attained by the ancient Greeks and in the musical field of melodic and harmonic counterpoint, the masterpieces that J.S. Bach composed in the 18th Century have yet to be surpassed. Likewise, from a rhythmic standpoint, the music that Nigerian and Congolese slaves brought to and further developed in Cuba over 500 years ago remains, even in the 21st Century, one of the most sophisticated and sublimely beautiful bodies of music ever created. Even in today's ultra-sophisticated musical world, many of the most brilliant and talented percussionists have devoted their lives to Afro-Cuban folkloric music. As for our faithful author, Tomás Cruz has studied and played all forms of Afro-Cuban folkloric music throughout his life and, like almost every other major figure in modern Cuban music, he cites this experience as perhaps the most important influence on his creative work. In Volume III we'll be able to see that a number of his original Timba marchas borrow and adapt musical ideas from folkloric music.

It's not an overstatement to say that it's virtually impossible to understand modern Cuban music without having a comfortable familiarity with its folkloric roots. Those who grow up in Cuba are surrounded from birth by the sounds and rhythms of their well-preserved musical heritage. Just as every American youngster can hum "The Star-Spangled Banner" and "Silent Night", the average Cuban child is equally familiar with the music of *Rumba* and *Batá*. The *Santería* religion is still widely practiced in Cuba, and even those of other faiths are very familiar with its musical culture, just as American Jews, Muslims and atheists are familiar with the songs and folklore of Christianity. *(photo: Tomás with Yoel Páez and friend at a casual Rumba party).*

The daunting subject of Afro-Cuban folkloric music can best be broken down into two large groups: the sacred and the secular. In addition to *Batá* music, the sacred category includes *Abacuá, Bakosó, Maíno, Asojano, Arará, Palo, Bríkamo,* and many other genres. Balancing the massive body of religious music is an equally impressive world of secular folkloric music including *Rumba, Comparsa, and Yuca.*

Afro-Cuban folkloric music and its application to modern conga drumming is a subject well worthy of its own 3-volume set and we hope to entice Tomasito to embark on such a project in the future, but for the purposes of this book, we asked him to give us a representative handful of marchas which are derived from folkloric music, which are of immediate use to the conguero in a popular music situation, and which had a direct effect on his own creative conga marchas.

Tomasito played with drummer Yoel Páez from 1996 to 1998. Páez later played with Issac Delgado and Manolín, el Médico de la Salsa. We consider him to be perhaps the most creative and tasteful drummer of the whole Timba genre.

For more on Yoel Páez, see http://yoelpaez.timba.com.

Marcha 1 – *Guaguancó* – DVD Chapters 1 & 2
2-3 Rumba Clave

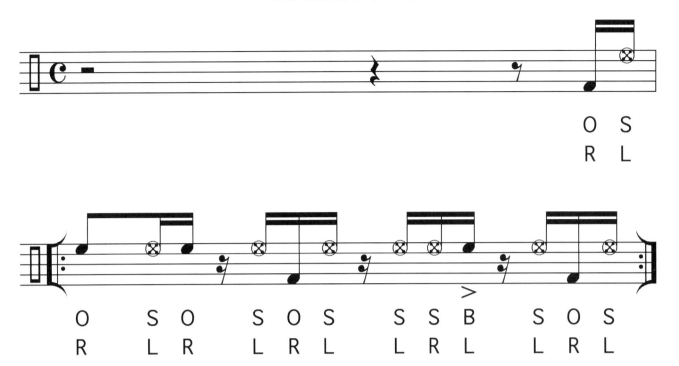

Of the Afro-Cuban folkloric rhythms, *Guaguancó* is by far the best-known outside of Cuba. It's made its way onto Cuban dance records, New York and Puerto Rican Salsa jams, countless Latin Jazz CD's, and even soul and funk tunes.

In its original form, Guaguancó is the most prevalent of the three principal rhythms of *Rumba,* the other two being the slower *Yambú* and the blazing fast, triple meter *Rumba Columbia.* In its native setting, Guaguancó is played by three drummers on three single congas. From largest to smallest, these are called the *tumbadora* or *salidor,* the *tres dos* or *segundo,* and the *quinto.* When the rhythm was adapted to the modern Latin ensemble the parts of the salidor and segundo were collapsed into the above marcha to enable a single conguero to play it on two drums in a band situation.

One of the most fascinating, influential and controversial aspects of the Guaguancó is the *"contraclave"* nature of its open tones. As explained in Appendix 2, the rhythms of some instruments in the Latin ensemble, particularly the kick drum and the congas, are sometimes constructed so as to intentionally contradict the clave. The first 3 open tones of the above Guaguancó marcha exactly follow the rhythmic shape of the 3-side of Son Clave, and yet the rhythm is played in 2-3 Rumba Clave. Older Cuban musicians attest to the fact that prior to the mid-1950's, 3-2 Clave *was* in fact used with the above rhythm. In fact, there even exist some very early recordings on which it was played this way by the most famous Rumba group, *"Los Muñequitos de Matanzas",* originally known as *"Conjunto Guaguancó Matancero".* Soon after, however, it became common practice in Cuba to play the Guaguancó *contraclave,* as Tomás plays it on the DVD, such that the open tones would echo the rhythm of the clave rather than coincide with it. In modern Cuban music such as Timba, this idea of aligning some instruments with the clave and pitting others against it became significantly more widespread. The conguero, like the other percussionists, needs to feel the clave at all times, but is sometimes expected to play parts which, taken by themselves, would seem to imply the opposite clave direction.

However, by the time the Cubans started playing it contraclave, the Guaguancó had already made its way to Puerto Rico, Colombia and New York, where even today some Salsa musicians continue to play the open tones with the clave instead of against it, preferring to reinforce the clave direction rather than counterbalance it. You'll probably find that in most situations you'll be expected to play "contraclave" as Tomasito does, but you should be able to play it the other way if called upon to do so.

Rumba is also played differently in Havana and Matanzas. The version shown above is played in the Havana style, the one normally adapted to band situations. The main difference in the Matanzas style is the absence of the second open tone.

Rumba is still a very vital part of the live music scene in Havana and continues to evolve. A case in point is a new type of Rumba known as *Guarapachangeo*, made famous by Los Chinitos of Habana Vieja. Guarapachangeo is a heightened and distilled style in which each of the three main percussionists plays a number of congas, batás, and/or cajones, each soloing within the parameters of their individual parts, somewhat analogous the group improvisation of Dixieland Jazz. Guarapachangeo arrangements can still be broken down into the three categories of Yambú, Guaguancó, and Rumba Columbia, but the dynamics of the interaction between the drummers changes. In traditional Rumba, the smallest conga, the *quinto,* does the bulk of the improvising while the supporting drums keep time and occasionally engage in predefined "conversations". In contrast, Guarapachangeo employs a model of collective improvisation and counterpoint. The two most virtuosic and creative Guarapachangeo groups in Cuba are Yoruba Andabo and Clave y Guaguancó.

Guaguancó – Recommended Listening

Traditional Guaguancó: An irresistible place to start is the compilation "**Los Muñequitos de Matanzas" (Tumbao Cuban Classics TCD 707)** by **Grupo Guaguancó Matancero**, whose first 78 rpm release had a B-side entitled *"Los Muñequitos de Matanzas",* a song which became so popular that people began calling the group itself by the same name. Los Muñequitos, now with different members, has recently celebrated its 50th anniversary. This CD compilation contains 17 tracks recorded between 1958 and 1963. Track 2, *"'Ta contento el pueblo",* is an example of the early Cuban rumberos playing the congas *with* the clave as described earlier. The rest of the tracks are *contraclave.* Rumba connoisseurs consider this early period to be the best period of Los Muñequitos, although any of the dozens of CD's by this group will provide you with excellent examples of Matanzas style folkloric Rumba.

Guaguancó adapted to Timba: Many of the greatest Cuban recordings of the 90's and 00's contain Guaguancó sections. Three of Tomasito's recordings contain classic tracks incorporating this rhythm. Paulito FG's biggest hit, *"De La Habana",* from **"Con la conciencia tranquila" (Nueva Fania NF108)** uses it in the introduction, as does Manolín, el Médico de la Salsa's *"Pegaíto, Pegaíto",* originally recorded by conguero Alexis "Mipa" Cuesta on **"De buena fe" (EMI 21306),** and later by Tomasito in Miami on the blistering live recording, **"El puente" (Ciocan Music HMC2605).** Tomasito also played on *"De La Habana a Matanzas"* from Juan Ceruto's Los Van Van tribute album, **"Gracias Formell" (RMM RMD 82249).** Los Van Van recorded the song twice, including **"Ay Dios ampárame" (Caribe Productions 9475),** featuring conguero Manolo Labarrera. Perhaps the most scorching Timba Guaguancó is *"Ven Sirocco Ven"* recorded by Manolito y su Trabuco on **"Para que baile Cuba" (Eurotropical 8431588900222)** and featuring Tomasito's pal Evelio Ramos on congas.

Guaguancó adapted to New York Salsa: The New Yorkers and Puerto Ricans were just as cognizant of the possibilities for Guaguancó in Salsa. One particularly compelling example is Andy González' arrangement of Arsenio Rodriguez' composition *"Llora timbero"* from Manny Oquendo's **"Ritmo, sonido y estilo" (Montuno 422).**

Guaguancó adapted to Latin Jazz: There are literally thousands of examples of Guaguancó in Latin Jazz. One standout featuring the astounding conguero **Roberto Vizcaíno** is *"Los caminos"* from **Chucho Valdés: "Bele Bele en La Habana" (Blue Note 23082).**

Guarapachangeo: As mentioned, Guarapachangeo is one of the most exciting new developments in Cuban music. Highly recommended are **"El callejón de los rumberos" (SDL22103),** by **Yoruba Andabo** and **"Noche de la Rumba"** by **Clave y Guaguancó (TUMI 085).** The latter has a guest appearance by Changuito. An interesting example of Guarapachangeo without singing can be heard on **Grupo Exploración: "Drum Jam" (Bembe 2026-2).**

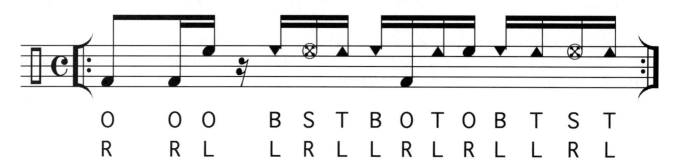

This marcha is one product of the 500 year journey of a family of rhythms from southwest Nigeria to the dance floors and concert halls of Havana, New York and Miami. *Iyesá* is the name of both a Nigerian ethnic group and a family of rhythms. Traditional Iyesá rhythms are played on four double-headed drums, two of which are played with sticks, one with a hand and a stick and the lowest with just the hands. Completing the Iyesá ensemble are two interlocking bell parts. There are two principal varieties of Iyesá, one in 4/4 (16th note feel) and one in "6/8" (triplet feel described in the next section). The original Iyesá is still performed and recorded in Cuba, and continues to be adapted for use in other Latin music contexts.

The Nigerians also brought another type of drum to Cuba, the *Batá*, whose family of rhythms is of paramount importance to Cuban music, both in terms of its influence on other Cuban genres and as a separate, enduring and evolving artform. We're hoping to entice Tomás to write additional volumes covering Batá drumming and its influence on the congas, but for the present book, we'll just say that the road to mastery of Cuban music most definitely passes through the beautiful and profound world of the Batá.

The *Oru del Igbodú*, or *Oru Seco* – the incredibly complex suite of liturgical rhythms which is used to begin each public Santería ceremony – is performed without vocals by only the three hour-glass shaped Batá drums. Later, the vocalists sing their tributes to the gods, or *Orishas*, accompanied by the Batás. The rhythms used to accompany these songs are many and varied and among the rhythms adapted by the *bataleros* was Iyesá. By the time they got through with it, however, Iyesá had gone through a considerable metamorphosis and the untrained ear is not likely to immediately hear striking similarities between the traditional Iyesá and the Batá rhythm of the same name.

It was while playing this adapted Iyesá rhythm on Batá that Tomasito became inspired to adapt it one step further and to develop the above conga marcha, which is based on the part of the largest Batá, the *Iyá*, filling in the unoccupied subdivisions with *manoteo* (see Volume I). While playing with the Timba supergroup Paulito FG y su Élite, Tomasito began to experiment with the rhythm during the more improvisational sections of the group's innovative "gear-based" arrangement system, which is one of the main subjects of Volume III of this series. The group's drummer, Yoel Páez (http://yoelpaez.timba.com), also a master of Batá drumming, would respond by incorporating elements of the middle Batá, the *Itótole*.

Iyesá and Batá – Recommended Listening

Traditional Iyesá: A great choice, and an excellent introduction to folkloric music in general, is **"Raíces Africanas" (Shanachie 66009)** by **Grupo AfroCuba de Matanzas.** This is a beautiful record with a great selection of authentically played folkloric rhythms, including *Guaguancó, Rumba Columbia, Bantú, Arará, Bríkamo,* some examples of *Batá* music, and much more.

Iyesá adapted to Batá: The Batá adaptation of Iyesá can be heard on **"Santísimo" (Luz Productions 001).** There are also versions by the Grammy-winning folkloric singer Lázaro Ros, but as of this writing none was currently in print. Perhaps the best way to keep up with the frequently changing catalog of folkloric recordings is to regularly visit the excellent educational website, www.batadrums.com. Folkloric recordings can also be purchased at www.descarga.com, www.amazon.com, www.timba.com, www.half.com, and the retail chain Amoeba Records.

Traditional Batá in general: "Sacred Rhythms" (Bembe 2027), by **Grupo Ilu Aña**, is a gorgeous recording of the Oru Seco, along with seven Batá-accompanied songs to the Orishas. Each movement of the Oru Seco has a separate track number. The performance, featuring the legendary Regino Jiménez, is nothing short of sublime. Lázaro Ros has recorded an extensive 13-CD set which includes instrumental Batá recordings, *a capella* vocals, and a variety of songs with full Batá accompaniment, organized by Orisha. The CD's are available as a set or individually on **Unicornio Records.**

Batá adapted to Timba: In a larger sense, one could say that the whole genre of Timba is partially adapted from Batá music. Many of Tomasito's most imaginative folkloric-influenced marchas can be found on **"Con la conciencia tranquila" (Nueva Fania NF106)** by **Paulito FG y su Élite.**

Batá Instructional Recordings: John Amira and Steven Cornelius have written an excellent book on Batá called **"The Music of Santería" (White Cliffs Media, distributed internationally by Mel Bay).** The book includes a thorough history and a recorded performance of the Oru Seco which is also completely notated! Coauthor Orlando Fiol plays *Itótole* on the CD.

"6/8" Marchas

Originally, Afro-Cuban folkloric music was not notated – it was simply passed down "by ear" from generation to generation. To a great degree, this is still true. As explained in Appendix 1 of Volume I, attempts to notate even popular Cuban music have led to confusion and debate, and the situation gets significantly stickier in the field of folkloric music.

While Cuban popular music consists almost entirely of groups of four beats, each with four subdivisions, about half of Afro-Cuban folkloric rhythms have groups of four beats with three subdivisions. European-trained musicians in Cuba notated these rhythms with a 6/8 time signature, and the name and notation method both stuck. Even Cuban musicians who don't read music at all, and there are many, use the terms "six eight" and *"seis por ocho"* to describe these folkloric rhythms.

To further complicate matters, numerous *Batá* rhythms and some secular ones, like *Rumba Columbia*, straddle both duple and triple meters, somehow inhabiting a mutually beneficial zone in which both can coexist amicably. The following marchas, however, are in straight triple meter and it's important that you hear them that way!

Although many Westerners hear Cuban 6/8 rhythms as being in a waltz-like meter (i.e. "in 3"), most Cubans hear it as a duple meter divided into triplets. It's critical to learn folkloric music, and most definitely the following three marchas, in groups of 4 beats. To reinforce this, the 6/8 marchas use a special click track (see next page) which uses the Jam Block timbre, normally used for the clave, to play the main beats as they should be felt. The bell plays the "6/8 Bell" pattern. Note that this is occasionally written in 12/8 without the barline – actually a more accurate representation of the music – but 6/8 is by far the most common notation.

6/8 Click Track (as written in common practice)

main beats:

6/8 bell:

The following rhythm is called "6/8 Clave", but Tomasito preferred to use the more common "6/8 Bell" for his click track.

6/8 Clave (not used in click track)

The following notation is never used and is only included to be absolutely certain that the student understands how Tomasito is feeling the meter.

6/8 Click Track (as you need to learn to feel it)

main beats:

6/8 bell:

Tomás gives us 3 ways to play a triple meter marcha in a band situation with a single conguero. These can be mixed and matched. Common to all is the open low drum on the 3rd subdivision of the 1st & 3rd beats. Tomás calls Marcha 3 "6/8 básico" and Marchas 4 & 5 "variaciones". In terms of their folkloric origins, Marcha 3 is loosely related to *Bakosó*, Marcha 4 to *Bríkamo*, and Marcha 5 to *Palo*.

Marcha 3 – *6/8 #1* – DVD Chapters 5 & 6

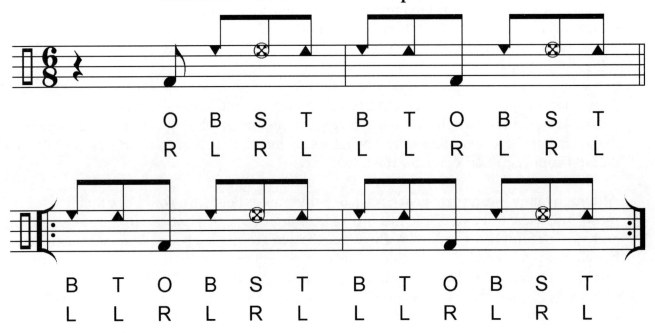

O	B	S	T	B	T	O	B	S	T
R	L	R	L	L	L	R	L	R	L

B	T	O	B	S	T	B	T	O	B	S	T
L	L	R	L	R	L	L	L	R	L	R	L

Marcha 4 – *6/8 #2* – DVD Chapters 7 & 8

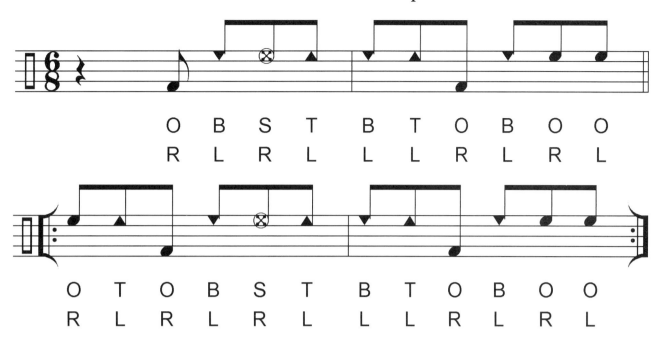

Marcha 5 – *6/8 #3* – DVD Chapters 9 & 10

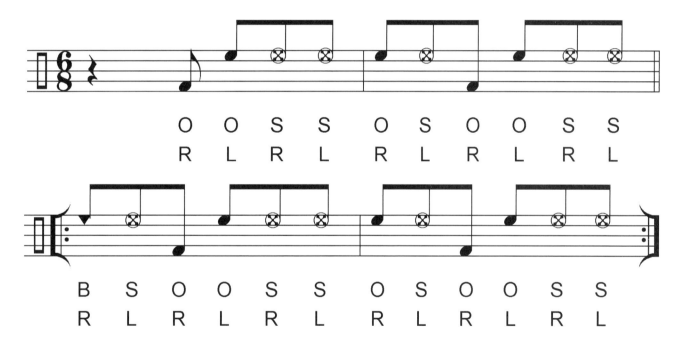

Why the Marchas Start Where They Do

Tomás and the other Cuban drummers we've encountered are all quite adamant about the correct starting point of each rhythm, and it often doesn't coincide with the "1" of the time signature, especially in these 6/8 marchas and in many of the *Timba* marchas in Volume III. Thus, in the DVD Chapters, you'll hear the click track go through a full cycle and begin again before the conga enters. See the Mozambique section for more on this.

6/8 – Recommended Listening

6/8 in folkloric music: Except for records containing all Guaguancó, almost any Afro-Cuban folkloric recording is likely to contain at least 50% rhythms in triple meter – for example the wonderful CD's already mentioned by Grupo Ilu Aña and Grupo AfroCuba de Matanzas.

6/8 adapted to Latin Jazz: Before listening to Latin Jazz with 6/8, we recommend getting very comfortable with feeling the 6/8 marcha "in 4" with triple meter as explained earlier. 6/8 is very common in Latin Jazz, and even in other Jazz, such as John Coltrane's recording of *"Afro-blue"*, and Miles Davis' *"Footprints"*. In the Jazz context, the bass and sometimes melody are often phrased such that the whole piece can sound like it's "in 3", or, in more sophisticated arrangements, that some of the instruments are in one meter and some in the other!

6/8 adapted to Salsa and Timba: While Guaguancó and the other duple meter folkloric rhythms have proved to be ideal candidates for fusion with popular Latin dance music like Salsa and Timba, 6/8 has fared less well. In contrast, the triple meter rhythms of English-language pop, sometimes called "shuffles", are a regular part of the rhythmic arsenal of everyone from B. B. King to the Beatles to Motown. The most likely reason for the failure of 6/8 to catch on in Latin pop is simply that, although there are plenty of folkloric dances in 6/8, all existing *popular* Latin dance styles are based on duple meter. Latin music and Latin dance are inextricably intertwined to the point that Juan Formell, one of Cuba's greatest composers, has said in interviews that he gets his ideas from watching people dance to his music. In any case, as of this writing, a "Latin shuffle" dance craze has yet to take the world by storm, so the use of 6/8 rhythms in Timba and Salsa is usually limited to intros, endings and short breakdowns. Such an example can be found on the extradordinary **"Juego de manos" (Eurotropical EUCD-3)** by **Klimax,** at the end of the song *"Lo mismo aquí que allá"*. Puerto Rican singer **Gilberto Santa Rosa** has actually been daring enough to record a few arrangements which switch back and forth between normal Salsa and 6/8, such as *Mala palabra* from **"De corazón" (Sony CDZ-82566/2-469924).** We've been very curious to see how U.S. dancers would try to dance to this one, but we haven't been able to convince any DJ to play it!

Changüí

Marcha Changüí – (not included on DVD)

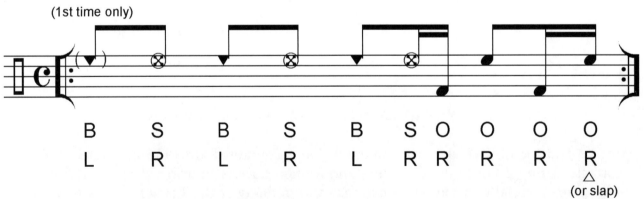

Changüí is a regional genre from Guantánamo which in spite of its rhythmic complexities is more immediately accessible to most listeners because of its use of a chord instrument to flesh out the harmonies. As the direct precursor to *Son*, it had a seminal influence on the development of Cuban popular music in the 20th century and even as of this writing, cutting edge groups such as Los Que Son Son, Manolito y su Trabuco and Klimax still draw on the flavor and vocabulary of Changüí. Tomasito says he sometimes uses this marcha in Timba to respond to a change to a *tres* or guitar timbre by the synthesizer player.

Like Son, the Changüí ensemble includes maracas, a güiro variant called a *guayo*, and the *tres*, a 3-stringed guitar-like instrument whose predominantly upbeat arpeggio patterns, called *paseos de calle*, eventually evolved into the modern piano tumbaos played in Salsa and Timba. In contrast to Son, however, Changüí is one of the few Cuban genres which doesn't adhere to a clave rhythm, because the tres patterns, which consist almost entirely of upbeats, can be repeated in odd length phrases which defy the binary rhythmic logic of the clave.

Son's use of the *bongó* was also anticipated by the larger and lower *bongó de monte*, whose characteristic phrases are the basis for the above conga marcha. (Neither Changüí nor Son uses congas in its traditional instrumentation).

The role of the bass in Changüí is played by a large kalimba-like instrument called the *marímbula*, whose characteristic part is the predecessor of the standard Salsa bass tumbao:

The term Changüí was adopted to describe the style of one of Cuba's most famous bands – Orquesta Revé, although the group doesn't use the Changüí instrumentation or rhythm patterns. Its founder, timbalero Elio Revé, formed the group before the Cuban Revolution and the group continues to be popular today under the leadership of pianist Elio Revé, Jr. Orquesta Revé was a spawning ground for many of the most important musicians in Cuban history including Juan Formell and César Pedroso, the main creative forces behind Los Van Van, and Chucho Valdés, the leader of Irakere.

Changüí – Recommended Listening

<u>Traditional Changüí</u>: **Grupo Changüí de Guantánamo**: **"La rumba está buena" (Disky DC 640752).** This is the leading traditional Changüí ensemble.

<u>Adaptation of Changüí</u>: **Grupo Exploración: "Drum Jam" (Bembe 2026-2).** This eclectic CD features creative modern compositions based on 16 different folkloric rhythms. The bongó parts on *"Ritmo Changüí"* are similar to Tomasito's Changüí marcha.

<u>Orquesta Revé</u>: **"Elio Revé y su Charangón, Vol. I and/or II" (Caribe Productions 9439 and 9440).**

PART 4: MARCHAS FROM OLDER CUBAN POP MUSIC

Marcha 6 – *Afro* – DVD Chapters 11 & 12

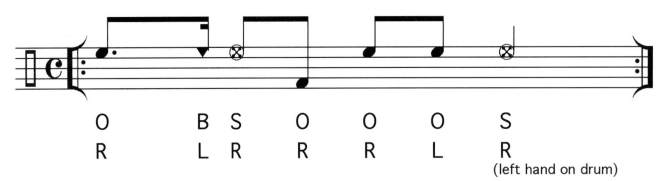

Afro – Recommended Listening

Three classic examples of the *Afro* rhythm are *"El yerbero moderno"* which can be found on **"At the Beginning" (Universal 160 150)** by **Celia Cruz**, *"Mata siguaraya"* from **"15 Éxitos de Beny Moré" (BMG 49061)** and *"Bruca manigua"* by **Arsenio Rodríguez**, from **"Quindembo" (Sony International B000002DYJ)**. Needless to say, there are much more important reasons to study these three legends of Cuban music beyond the fact that they recorded the relatively obscure Afro rhythm! Celia Cruz and Beny Moré are the most famous Cuban singers of the middle 20th Century, and for good reason, but from the point of view of our study of Cuban rhythms and musical forms, the most important of the three by a considerable margin is the man who introduced the conga to popular music, Arsenio Rodríguez.

An Introduction to Arsenio Rodríguez

If learning to appreciate Afro-Cuban folkoric music is challenging because of its complexity, the opposite problem can occur when studying the pop music of the middle 20th century, whether it be from Cuba or the United States. Rather than being difficult to understand, it can simply be difficult to *enjoy* until one acquires a taste for its potentially "old-fashioned" sounding rhythms, harmonies, lyrics, and recording quality. There is, however a handful of artists who are so primordially funky that modern ears can appreciate them immediately in spite of their vintage. In Jazz, Lester Young and Billie Holiday come to mind, but in Cuban music, the name to remember is **Arsenio Rodríguez,** the blind tres player/rumba drummer who completely revolutionized Cuban pop music in any number of absolutely pivotal ways. Rodríguez should be very near and dear to the reader's heart if for no other reason that it was he who introduced the conga to popular music. He also added the hand-held cowbell and introduced the piano to the Latin ensemble, adapting traditional tres patterns to create the first piano tumbaos, or *"montunos"*, as they were called prior to 1990. But the most important contribution of the genius of Arsenio Rodríguez went well beyond orchestration. Setting the tone for Juan Formell and the Timberos who came decades later, Rodríguez intuitively understood that new European harmonic influences needed to be accompanied by new African rhythmic influences in order to maintain the balance that makes Cuban music so unique. With the genres of *Danzón, Contradanza, Bolero,* and *Son,* the Cuban music of the late 19th and early 20th centuries had experienced a massive influx of new harmonic ideas. It was Rodríguez who put the *montuno* in *Son Montuno* – by infusing rhythmic elements from Rumba and transforming the previously negligible "montuno" sections to feature fiery horn mambos and instrumental solos.

Although it doesn't contain *"Bruca manigua"*, the best overall compilation of Arsensio Rodríguez recordings is probably **"Leyendas" (Sony 81534/2-469742)**.

Special Dengue Click Track

Who, you may ask, would want to name a rhythm after a deadly virus? Were he still alive, the man to ask would be Pérez Prado, a bandleader who sustained a very successful show business career by introducing the global market to a series of dance crazes based on somewhat watered down Cuban rhythms, the most famous being the *"Mambo"*. He created the extremely short-lived *Dengue* dance craze to coincide with the release of a musical comedy entitled *"El Dengue del Amor"*, in which he also co-starred.

To avoid confusion, it should be noted that for the conguero in today's playing situations, the term *"mambo"* has a very different meaning, referring to the high-energy brass sections which alternate with call and response vocals in the typical Salsa/Timba arrangement format. If the bandleader calls out "Mambo!", please do *not* switch to the Dengue marcha! As you'll see in Volume III, the horn mambo section requires an intensification of the conga marcha and often requires the conguero and other percussionists to add soloistic fills in response to the phrases of the horns.

Mozambique

Unrelated to the African country of the same name, the *Mozambique* genre was created by Cuban singer/composer/percussionist Pello el Afrokán in the early 1960's in an effort to modernize the folkloric *carnaval* rhythm known as *comparsa* or *conga* and make it suitable for use with melodic instruments in popular dance ensembles.

Tomás created his own unquantized click track for this rhythm, with a 2-3 Rumba clave orientation, like most if not all of Pello el Afrokán's recordings. As explained earlier, Tomás and other Cuban musicians have very strong feelings about where their patterns begin, and this is another case where the conga entrance is different from the "1" of the harmonic and melodic instruments. To hear how this works in actual practice, refer to Pello el Afrokán's famous *"Ileana quiere chocolate"*, from the recommended recording at the end of this section. The congas enter, as Tomasito does, on the 3-side; then the bells enter on the 2-side; and finally the song begins, with its musical phrases clearly beginning on the 2-side. In today's Timba, a similar overlapping effect occurs when the congas *and* bells enter on the 2-side in songs whose musical phrases begin on the 3-side. It can be difficult conceptually to learn to enter this way, but the end result is very effective and takes on a funky logic of its own.

Special Mozambique Click Track

small bell:

campana:

toms:

Marchas 8 & 9 are distillations of the two most common conga parts in the Mozambique ensemble and are really meant to be played together by two congueros. Marcha 10 is a variation of Marcha 8.

Marcha 8 – *Mozambique #1* – DVD Chapters 15 & 16
2-3 Rumba Clave

Marcha 9 – *Mozambique #2* – DVD Chapters 17 & 18
2-3 Rumba Clave

Marcha 10 – *Mozambique #3* – DVD Chapters 19 & 20
2-3 Rumba Clave

Finally, Marcha 11 is Tomasito's original combination of Mozambique with a normal Salsa tumbao. Today, rhythms like Mozambique, Dengue and Afro are seldom played in their original forms, but are part of a vast common vocabulary of earlier rhythms to which today's generation of Cuban musicians refer, both consciously and subconsciously, as inspiration for their own musical creativity.

Tomasito devised a click track which switches between the Mozambique rhythm and a straight *cáscara* with 2-3 Rumba Clave.

Marcha 11 – Original Adaptation of Mozambique – DVD Chapters 21 & 22
2-3 Rumba Clave

Mozambique – Recommended Listening and Further Study

An excellent compilation of Pello el Afrokán's best work is **"Nace en Cuba el Mozambique"** **(Orfeon CDL-16175)**. For further study, Kim Atkinson of PulseWave Percussion has produced an entire video course dealing exclusively with the Cuban Mozambique and a companion video which covers the genre of the same name which developed in New York. Note that all the marchas presented in *this* book refer to the Cuban variety.

Marcha 12 – *Pilón* – DVD Chapters 23 & 24
3-2 Son Clave

The adaptation of the *Pilón* rhythm to later forms such as Timba provides a great example of the continuity that seems to exist between generations of Cuban musicians. As in any culture, older Cubans are not always completely in tune with, or in approval of, the innovations of their youthful counterparts, but *unlike* most other cultures, each generation of young Cuban musicians seems to have an unusual degree of reverence for the past and a surprising amount of knowledge about the overall history of the country's music. As such, our observation is that Cuban music has grown very organically from *Batá, Rumba, Danzón* and *Changüí* to *Son*, to *Son Montuno*, to *Songo*, and to *Timba* and beyond.

Pilón is a name for a type of large vat in which coffee beans are roasted, and the dance of the same name imitates the rotating movement of stirring the beans with a long pole. The dance and its accompanying rhythm were popularized in the 1960's by Pacho Alonso. The timbales play a pattern derived from the bongó marchas used to accompany tres solos in *Son* and *Guaracha,* and the bell pattern resembles the steady pulse of the güiro in *Charanga,* but the conga pattern is quite unique. After Pacho Alonso's son Pachito took over the band in the 1990's, Tomasito's friend and colleague Orlando Mengual was hired to play congas. Mengual came from the same musical family which produced the famous *Rumba* group, "Los Papines". Mengual began to create his own variants of the Pilón rhythm which he used not only when the band was doing a nostalgic updated Pilón, but also in breakdown sections of Salsa and Timba arrangements. When he later joined "La Charanga Habanera", one of the most innovative Timba bands, he was able to create even more adventurous Pilón variants. Thus, through musicians like Mengual, rhythmic building blocks from *Rumba, Pilón,* many other earlier genres became a fertile foundation for the exciting new developments of subsequent generations. The Pilón rhythm was adapted in quite a different way by another of the great congueros of Tomasito's generation, Denis *"Papacho"* Savón, who can as of this writing be seen touring with Issac Delgado.

Pilón – Recommended Listening

The original Pacho Alonso hit, *"Rico Pilón"*, can be found on the album of the same name **(BIS 041)**, but on the whole, a better choice might be Pachito Jr.'s 1994 release, **Pachito Alonso y su Kini Kini: "¡Yo siempre tengo lo que tú necesitas!" (Caribe Productions 9427),** which features an updated version of *"Rico Pilón"*, including a section with the original Pilón groove, and which also features the exciting conga work of Orlando Mengual and a number of other musicians who would go on to become famous in their own right with other groups. To hear Mengual's Pilón adaptations in a pure *Timba* setting, try **"Live in the USA" (Ciocan 62606-2)** by **Charanga Habanera.** One of many examples of the Pilón-influenced conga marchas comes near the beginning of *"Ya está bueno de bla, bla, bla"* among many other places. A studio recording of the same group is **"Charanguero mayor" (JMI 001).**

Marcha 13 – *Suku Suku* – DVD Chapters 25 & 26
2-3 Son Clave

Like Pilón, the origins of *Suku Suku* are in the *Oriente,* the far Eastern tip of Cuba, especially in and around Santiago. On the surface, it resembles the often used *a caballo* rhythm that imitates the galloping of a horse, but once the basic hand pattern is understood this rhythm offers many possibilities for development. Unlike most *manoteo*-based marchas, the slaps of the Suku Suku rhythm fall on the downbeats instaad of the upbeats. The triple stroke with the left hand results in the rhythm usually being played at slow to moderate tempi.

Suku Suku – Recommended Listening

The most famous Suku Suku is a recording of Silvio Rodríguez' *"Cántalo pero baílalo"* by **Adalberto Álvarez y su Son,** one of the most successful pre-Timba bands of the 80's and one which is still popular today. *"Cántalo pero baílalo"* can be found on **"Grandes Éxitos" (EGREM CD0280).**

PART 5: SONGO

The genre that best symbolizes post-Revolutionary Cuba to the rest of the world is *Songo*. The term was coined by one of Cuba's greatest musical visionaries, Juan Formell, to describe the music of his group, Los Van Van. By 1969, The Beatles, Motown and others had drastically raised the standards for popular music and Formell realized that to fully participate in that creative revolution, he would have to first dismantle the system of harmonic and stylistic limitations that had previously defined the boundaries of "Latin" songwriting. In 1969 he left his post as musical director of Orquesta Revé, taking along a nucleus of Revé's musicians, and formed Los Van Van as a vehicle for his musical experiments, which continue as of this writing, and which have allowed Formell and Van Van to miraculously stay at the top of the charts and at the cutting edge of Cuban music for well over 30 years. Formell's alter-ego, pianist César "Pupy" Pedroso, has consistently balanced Formell's eclectic compositions with his own darker, grittier masterpieces – more firmly grounded in tradition – resulting in a songwriting tandem that, like almost everything else about Los Van Van, is unparalleled in Cuban music. In 2001, Pedroso left to form his own group, Los Que Son Son, but Formell, 61 years of age as of this writing, has retooled with young musicians and continues to write innovative new music, not only for Los Van Van, but for other groups such as Issac Delgado and Charanga Forever.

From a rhythmic standpoint, Songo's chief architect was none other than Tomasito's teacher, José Luis "Changuito" Quintana. Changuito played drums and timbales with Los Van from 1970 until the early 1990's. Los Van Van's first conguero, whom Changuito credits with inventing the first Songo conga rhythm, was the late Raúl "El Yulo" Cárdenas. El Yulo left in about 1980 and was replaced briefly by Joel Drigs and then by Manolo Labarrera, who is still with the group today.

The other important group that is often included in the Songo category is Ritmo Oriental, although the group itself calls its music *"Nueva Onda"*. It was founded in the late 50's and still exists today, although its most innovative decades were the 70's and 80's. Ritmo Oriental took the basic format of *Charanga* to new heighths with creative arrangements featuring, among other things, one of the band's musical trademarks, the "photo-op freeze". The band would play a break at a ritarded tempo and the dancers would freeze in place, but only for the slightest instant before the band and dancers would surge back into tempo with exhilirating grace. Among the many musicians to start out with "La Ritmo" were Tony Calá, who would later sing in the first Timba band, NG La Banda, and David Calzado, who became the leader of the second great Timba band, and still one of the most influential, La Charanga Habanera.

Marcha 14 – *Songo básico* – DVD Chapters 27 & 28
2-3 Rumba Clave

This most basic Songo marcha repeats after two beats. It differs from a standard salsa tumbao in that the two consecutive bass strokes allow the open tones to be moved to the big drum and an offbeat left hand slap to be inserted in place of the tip. This marcha is often played very rapidly, as in Tomasito's recommended listening examples, *"Yo bailo de todo"* and *"La chica mamey"* from **"La Historia de la Ritmo, Volume I" (QBADisc QB 9007)** by **Ritmo Oriental.**

Marcha 15 – *Songo #2* – DVD Chapters 29 & 30
2-3 Rumba Clave

Marcha 15 is one of the more complex Songo variations, and can be studied after Marchas 16 through 18 if desired. The first beat, like *Songo básico,* is picoteo (see Vol. 1). This is followed by a melodic series of open tones and then, the most interesting feature, two slaps which accent the 3-side of the clave, such that when the marcha loops around, three consecutive strokes of Rumba Clave are played by slaps. Listen carefully to the clave when you practice this one.

Marcha 15 can be heard in Los Van Van's recordings from the early 70's, on songs like *"Ponte para las cosas"* and *"Uno solo fuerte"*, both from **Colección, Volume II (EGREM CD0127)**. It's particularly easy to hear on *"Uno solo fuerte"*, which begins with layered percussion.

Marcha 16 – *Songo #3* – DVD Chapters 31 & 32
2-3 Rumba Clave

Variations of Marcha 16 are used on Ritmo Oriental's *"Cuidado con la percusión"*, which can be found on the compilation **Cuban Gold, Volume II (QBADISC 9016).**

Note that when the pattern repeats, it's necessary to play open, bass, and then tip, all with the left hand. Watch the DVD carefully to see how Tomasito throws his left hand forward to make the transition from the open to the bass. One alternative way to play this pattern which avoids the problem of playing three strokes in a row with the same hand is to change the first stroke to a right hand bass and the second stroke to a left hand slap:

B	S	S	B	B	S	O	O	B	O	B	T	O	S	O	O
R	L	R	L	R	L	R	R	L	R	L	L	R	L	R	L

A second alternative is to change the first stroke to a right hand ghost and the second to a left hand bass:

G	B	S	B	B	S	O	O	B	O	B	T	O	S	O	O
R	L	R	L	R	L	R	R	L	R	L	L	R	L	R	L

These handing substitutions can be used whenever a marcha ends on a left hand stroke. It's a matter of personal choice and Tomasito uses them all interchangeably.

Marcha 17 – *Songo #4* – DVD Chapters 33 & 34
2-3 Rumba Clave

B	T	S	B	B	S	O	O		O	O	O	O	O	O	O
L	L	R	L	R	L	R	R		L	R	L	R	L	R	L

The most common and recognizable difference between Songo marchas and the standard Salsa tumbao is that the two open tones normally played on the quinto are moved to the low drum so that the quinto can be used to create melodic variations like those in Marcha 17. After you master this one, trying inventing your own variations. Play the first two beats as written and then improvise with open tones on beats 3 & 4.

Marcha 18 – *Songo #5* – DVD Chapters 35 & 36
2-3 Rumba Clave

B T S B B S O O B O B T B S O O
L L R L R L R R L R L L R L R R

Variations of this marcha can be heard on one of Ritmo Oriental's most famous songs, *"El baile del azúcar"*, sometimes called *"Baila azúcar"*, which can be found on **"Guarachando" (ARTEX 55).** After leaving Ritmo Oriental to form the Timba group Charanga Habanera, David Calzado re-recorded the song on the CD **"El baile del azúcar" (Rosita 208).**

The only difference between Marcha 18 and Marcha 14, *Songo básico,* is the open quinto tone which occurs on the second subdivision of the third beat. This rhythmic location is frequently accented by the quinto in Rumba, and later become a common way for the kick drum to mark the 3-side in Timba. Thus, while Marcha 14 is clave-neutral, it's important to play Marcha 18 so that the quinto tone falls on the 3-side of the clave.

Marcha 19 – *Songo #6* – *Songo con marcha 1* – DVD Chapters 37 & 38
2-3 Rumba Clave

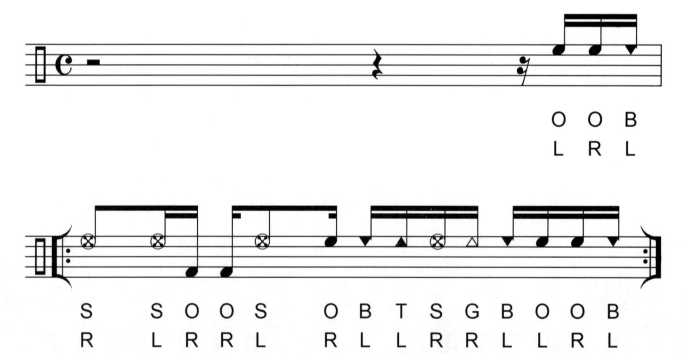

Marcha 20 – *Songo #7 – Songo con marcha 2* – DVD Chapters 39 & 40
2-3 Rumba Clave

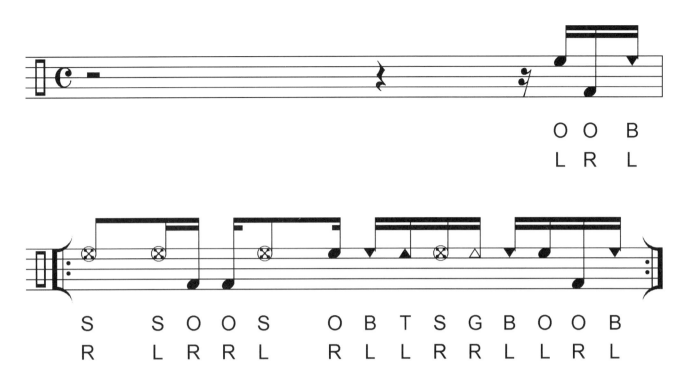

Tomasito calls Marchas 19 and 20 *"Songo con marcha"*. The distinctive slaps on the 2-side are borrowed from one of Los Van Van's most popular marchas (Marcha 21).

Marcha 21 – *Songo #8* – DVD Chapters 41 & 42
3-2 Rumba Clave

Marcha 21 was used extensively in the late 80's and early 90's by Los Van Van's current conguero, Manolo Labarrera. Perhaps the most famous example is on the title track of **"Disco Azúcar" (Xenophile GLCD 4025),** which also happens to be the final recording Changuito made with the group. The song also appears on **"The Legendary Los Van Van – 30 Years of Cuba's Greatest Dance Band" (Ashé CD 2007 A & B).**

Note that the two consecutive slaps mark the 2-side of the clave. The DVD chapter is played with a 3-2 Rumba Clave click track, corresponding to the song *"Disco Azúcar"*. In contrast, Marchas 19 & 20 use a 2-3 click track, so the slaps are played on the first half instead.

Variations of this marcha are also used on *"Nosotros los del Caribe"* and *"La titimanía"*, the first two tracks of **Colección, Volume XII (EGREM CED0137)**. *"La titimanía"*, also appears on **"The Legendary Los Van Van – 30 Years of Cuba's Greatest Dance Band" (Ashé CD 2007 A & B)**.

Other Los Van Van tracks using this marcha are *"Anda, muévete y ven"* from **Colección, Volume IX (EGREM CD0134)**, and *"Esto está bueno"* from **Colección, Volume XV (EGREM CD0140)** and **"The Legendary Los Van Van – 30 Years of Cuba's Greatest Dance Band" (Ashé CD 2007 A & B)**.

Marcha 22 – *Songo #9* – DVD Chapters 43 &44
2-3 Rumba Clave

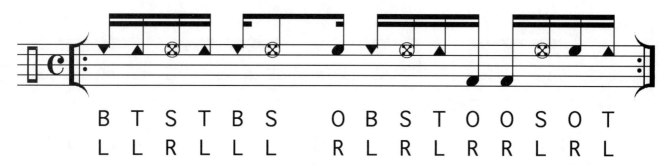

Marcha 22 is used on the most famous Los Van Van song of the pre-Timba era, *"Por encima del nivel"*, also called *"Sandunguera"*, from **Colección, Volume XIII (EGREM CD0133)** and **"The Legendary Los Van Van – 30 Years of Cuba's Greatest Dance Band" (Ashé CD 2007 A & B)**.

Marcha 23 – *Merensongo* – DVD Chapters 45 & 46
3-2 Rumba Clave

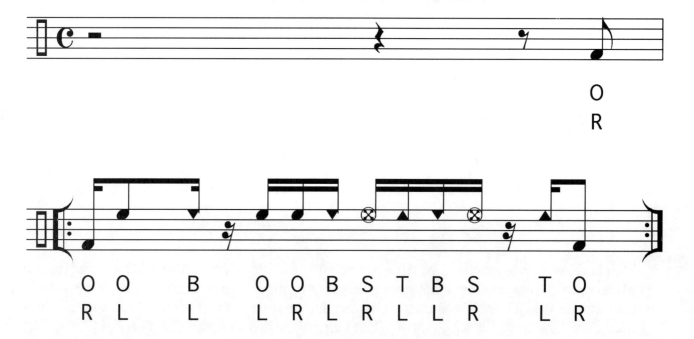

Changuito's famous *Merensongo* rhythm incorporates elements of the Dominican *Merengue* rhythm studied in the next section. It can be heard on *"Quien bien la quiere te hará llorar"* **Colección, Volume X (EGREM CED0135)**.

Songo – Recommended Listening

Los Van Van

Los Van Van's 33 year history can be divided into two parts. The first 15 albums were originally released only on vinyl LP's and were later reissued by EGREM as the 15-CD **"Colección"** series **(EGREM CD 0126 through CD 0140)**. The recording quality is primitive by modern standards, but "Colección" is the only practical way to collect the first 20 years of Los Van Van's history in its entirety. The volumes are available separately and correspond chronologically to the vinyl LP's released in the 70's and 80's.

In the 90's the group released five more CD's, each a major milestone of the Timba era. These have significantly better recording quality and are indispensable to any Timba collection: **"Disco Azúcar" (Xenophile GLCD 4025), "Lo último en vivo" (Qbadisc QB 9020), "Ay Dios, ampárame" (Caribe 9075), "Te pone la cabeza mala" (Caribe 9506),** and **"Llegó Van Van" (Havana Caliente 83227-2).** Changuito left the group after "Disco Azúcar" and was replaced by Juan Formell's son Samuel, an extremely exciting musician in his own right.

If you're looking for a "greatest hits" approach, there are dozens of confusing compilations. The best is undoubtedly a beautifully remastered 2-CD retrospective of Los Van Van's career called **"The Legendary Los Van Van – 30 Years of Cuba's Greatest Dance Band" (Ashé CD 2007 A & B).** The first disc covers the biggest hits of the first 20 years, with greatly enhanced audio quality, and Disc 2 is devoted to the albums of the 90's, although it's impossible to do justice to this decade in a single disc. The package also includes a 106-page bilingual booklet with a full history of the band's personnel, lyrics in both languages, and liner notes by the brilliant pianist/composer Rebeca Mauleón-Santana, author of many ground-breaking educational books on Latin music. Rebeca also collaborated with Changuito on a video called **"The History of Songo" (DCI VH0277)**, which is an excellent resource for further study of Songo.

Ritmo Oriental

As with Los Van Van, there's one compilation which stands out as the best: **"Historia de La Ritmo" (Qbadisc QB 9007 & QB 9008).** It's also a 2-CD set, but each volume can be bought separately. Volume II features the participation of Tony Calá and David Calzado but Volume I features many of the group's greatest hits.

Marchas 24 through 26 – *Bota*

Bota is a Songo rhythm that Changuito frequently used in the introduction and breakdown sections of Los Van Van arrangements. A key rhythmic feature is the accenting of both offbeat 16[ths] of the second and fourth beats.

As we'll see in Volume III, the Bota rhythm had an important influence on Tomasito's style. One of the main advancements of Timba was the use of specific rhythm section modes, or "gears", which could be built into the arrangement, or spontaneously invoked by hand signals in live performance. This reached its highest level in the extraordinary Paulito FG group of 1998, Tomasito's last group before moving to Miami. One of the most exciting "gears" of that band was Songo con efectos, with conga parts that were build arround the Bota rhythm. Tragically, as a result of Tomasito's move to Miami before the group recorded again, there are no commercial recordings of the Songo con efectos gear. However, as a special bonus for true fanatics of Timba conga-playing, we've included a Songo con efectos tutorial in Appendix 3 on page 82.

Returning to the Bota rhythm itself (which was recorded extensively by Los Van Van), Tomasito gives us three variations which can be used interchangeably and lend themselves to improvisation.

Marcha 24 – *Bota básico* – DVD Chapters 47 & 48
2-3 Rumba Clave

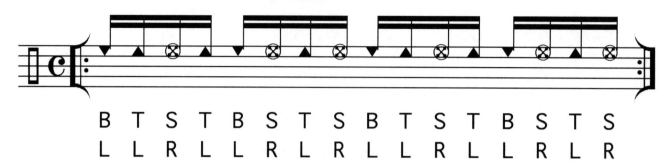

B	T	S	T	B	S	T	S	B	T	S	T	B	S	T	S
L	L	R	L	L	R	L	R	L	L	R	L	L	R	L	R

Marcha 25 – *Bota #2* – DVD Chapters 49 & 50
2-3 Rumba Clave

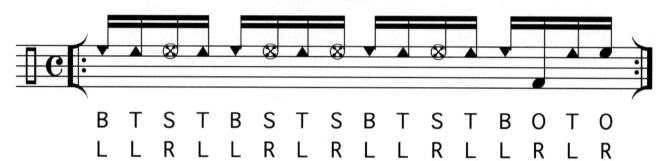

B	T	S	T	B	S	T	S	B	T	S	T	B	O	T	O
L	L	R	L	L	R	L	R	L	L	R	L	L	R	L	R

Marcha 26 – *Bota #3* – DVD Chapters 51 & 52
2-3 Rumba Clave

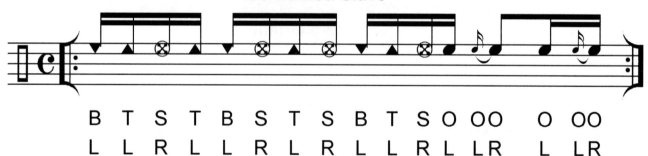

B	T	S	T	B	S	T	S	B	T	S	O	O	OO	O	OO
L	L	R	L	L	R	L	R	L	L	R	L	L	LR	L	LR

Bota #3 is also often played using the tumba:

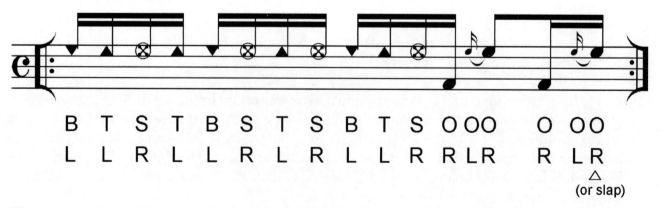

B	T	S	T	B	S	T	S	B	T	S	O	O	OO	O	OO
L	L	R	L	L	R	L	R	L	L	R	R	R	LR	R	LR

△
(or slap)

Clear examples of Bota can be heard in the introductions to the following: **Los Van Van: Colección, Volume XIV (EGREM CED0139):** *"Se cambia el turno" and "Tranquilo Mota";* **Colección, Volume XV (EGREM CED0140):** *"Que no me mires más así".*

PART 6: MARCHAS FROM NON-CUBAN RHYTHMS
Merengue
Marcha 27 – *Merengue* – DVD Chapters 53 & 54

Merengue, currently one of the most popular dance rhythms worldwide, originated in the Dominican Republic although many leading Merengue artists of the last 15 years are from Puerto Rico and New York. It's still sometimes played in its original form, *Perico ripiao,* using an instrumentation of only accordion, a metal *güira,* a double-headed *tambora* drum and sometimes bass and/or saxophone.

Modern commercial Merengue adds piano, a full horn section, and congas. The first Dominican congueros experimented with the use of various Afro-Cuban conga rhythms to complement the basic tambora rhythm. Most settled on a relatively simple adaptation of the generic tumbao because of the extremely fast tempos involved. In the mid-80's, however, the marcha played by Tomasito in the DVD chapter, more influenced by traditional Puerto Rican rhythms, became the conga pattern of choice.

Marcha 28 – *Merengue Apambichao* – DVD Chapters 55 & 56

Pambiche, or *Merengue Apambichao,* a variation of the traditional Merengue, can be heard in its original form (without congas) in the song *"Juanito Morel"* from the *Perico Ripiao* listening recommendation below. The marcha Tomasito plays on the DVD is a loose adaption of this rhythm to the congas.

The "Cubanization" process moved a step further from the source when Alexis "Mipa" Cuesta, Tomasito's predecessor in the Médico de la Salsa group, started experimenting improvisationally with elements of the Ampambichao rhythm. Tomasito developed the idea further by creating compositionally conceived two-measure marchas which only make reference to the original Apambichao every other bar. An example is *Marcha Apambichao* from Volume III of this series. The brackets show the similarity to Marcha 28 on the previous page.

It's hard to imagine two *less* similar pieces of music than the first and fourth listening examples on the following page: Tatico Henríquez' traditional version of *"Juanito Morel"* and Tomasito's live performance of *"No lo comentes"* from Manolín's *"El Puente".* And yet, we can now see that they share an important rhythmic bloodline, just as Charanga Habanera's and Issac Delgado's funky Timba breakdowns incorporate elements of the *Pilón,* as Paulito FG's ultra-sophisticated *songo con efectos* gear is rooted in the *Bota* rhythm from the *Songo* genre, and as almost all modern Cuban music is inextricably linked to *Rumba* and *Batá.*

Thus, while on the surface this book seems to be a logical sequel to the beginning conga lessons of Volume I, we actually conceived it as a *prequel* to Volume III. In Volume III, Tomasito explains *what* he plays in today's exciting modern Cuban music; in the present volume, he shows us where at least some of it came from – revealing the common rhythmic vocabulary which provided the launching pad for the quantum leaps of Tomasito and his generation of congueros.

Merengue – Recommended Listening

Traditional Perico Ripiao: (no congas) **Tatico Henríquez, "El Disco de Oro" (Kubaney CD 1347)** *("Juanito Morel"* is an excellent example of traditional *Pambiche.)*

Modern popular Merengue: (with congas) **La Makina, "Los Reyes del Ritmo" (Sony International B000001AS2)**

Merengue adapted to Cuban Songo: See Merensongo in Part 6.

Merengue Apambichao adapted to Timba: *"No lo comentes"* from **Manolín, El Médico de la Salsa, "El Puente" (Ciocan Music HMC2605)** (Tomasito's part at about 3:00 is based on the marcha on the previous page.) Manolín was the most popular artist in Cuba in the second half of the 90's before running into trouble with the government and defecting to the United States. Tomasito joined the group when it reformed in Miami. "El puente" is a live double album recorded with Reinier Guerra playing drums and Tomás on congas. Tomás later overdubbed the güiro parts in the studio. While the connection between Manolín's music and Merengue Apambichao is extremely subtle, this historic live concert is a powerful example of Tomasito's playing and of the Timba genre which will be studied in depth in Volume III of this series.

Bomba

Puerto Rican music, like that of Cuba and the Domincan Republic, is dominated by rhythms originally brought from Africa. Among the many forms of *Afro-Boricuan* folkloric music, the two which are most frequently adapted to the congas in popular music are *Bomba* and *Plena*. While Plena is currently experiencing a rebirth in popularity in New York and Puerto Rico in the work of such groups as Plena Libre, it's been Bomba which has had the biggest influence on Cuban music.

The traditional Bomba ensemble includes the *cuá*, consisting of two sticks played on a wooden log or other hard surface, a single maraca, and two or more barrel-shaped drums which look like short, fat congas. The player of the smaller lead drum, the *primo* or *salidor*, improvises in response to the movements of the dancers while one or more supporting drummers, depending on the region and style, keep time on the larger *buleador* drums.

The rhythm adapted to the congas in Marchas 29 and 30 is usually called simply "Bomba", but it's based specifically on *Bomba Sicá*, which is only one facet of the massive Bomba genre. There are many other types of Bomba, such as *Yubá, Holandé,* and *Lerú*. The idea of adapting Bomba Sicá to the congas and to popular music in general is usually credited to Puerto Rican bandleader Rafael Cortijo and singer Ismael Rivera.

The powerful influence of Bomba on Cuban Timba began in 1989 when NG La Banda, the first Timba band, used the rhythm on several songs from the seminal "En la calle" album. NG la Banda was also the first to create a special "gear" combining elements of Bomba with a bass style that involved sliding the right hand down the lowest string. The approach used by NG was then personalized and further developed by most other Timba bands. The "rhythm section gear" connotation of the word "Bomba" is investigated in depth in Volume III. For now, we suggest that you learn the two marchas given here, which will come in handy in a variety of playing situations, but also consider further exploring both its folkloric roots and its later permutations in the world of Timba.

Marcha 29 – *Bomba 1* – DVD Chapters 57 & 58

M S O O S
R L R R L

S B T M S O O S O   O M S O O S
R L L R L R R L R   L R L R R L

Since Bomba is clave-neutral, the DVD chapters use the following click track:

bell:

woodblock:

Plena

Plena developed in Ponce, in the southern part of Puerto Rico, and was originally played on large tambourine-shaped instruments called *pandaretas*. It's currently very popular in New York and Puerto Rico although it hasn't yet had a major impact on Cuban music. Tomás didn't record a DVD chapter for Plena, but it's a good rhythm to have on hand for many professional playing situations. It's shown here in 2-3 clave.

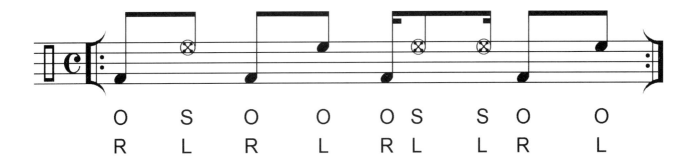

O S O O O S S O O
R L R L R L L R L

Bomba and Plena – Recommended Listening

Afro-Boricuan Folkloric Bomba: Los Hermanos Ayala: "Ballet Folklórico" (Casabe 727-1); Grupo Afro-Boricua: "Bombazo" (Blue Jackel 5027); Paracumbé: "Tambó" (Ashé CD 2005); Cepeda Family: "Dancing the Drum" (Bembe 2028). These use the original Bomba instruments (no congas) and cover a wide range of Bomba rhythms from the various regions of Puerto Rico. A great video, in Spanish without subtitles, is **"Raíces" (Banco Popular BPPR-2001-VHS).**

Bomba (and Plena) adapted to Puerto Rican Popular Music: Cortijo y su Combo with Ismael Rivera: "24 Éxitos de Cortijo y su Combo" (Fuentes 16114). Note that Cortijo didn't record Bombas exclusively and some compilations have tracks which are mislabeled "Bomba" or "Plena", but which are actually normal Guarachas. This particular compilation is an excellent one in that it has numerous examples of each rhythm and also features the legendary singer Ismael Rivera.

Bomba adapted to Timba: The following are examples of Timba recordings which adapt Bomba to the main sections of the arrangement: *"No se puede tapar el sol"* and *"To' el mundo e' bueno, camará"* from **NG La Banda: "En la calle" (Qbadisc QB9002).** This CD is a compilation drawn from what were essentially the first Timba LP's ever recorded. It also features the famous conguero Juan "Wickly" Nogueras, who, like Tomasito, now lives in Miami. Another indispensable Timba classic is **Klimax: "Mira si te gusta" (Eurotropical MACD-17).** The title track is a Bomba, but the whole record, and its conguero, Jorge Luis "Papiosco" Torres, are well worth studying for many other reasons as well. Papiosco can currently be heard with the touring band, Cubanismo.

The Bomba "Gear" in Timba: Paulito FG: "Con la conciencia tranquila" (Nueva Fania NF 108). This album (see below) uses the hybrid Timba Bomba "gear" on nearly every song. Many experts call "Con la conciencia" the greatest Cuban album of the 90's, and it was the fascination with this modern masterpiece that led the coauthors to seek out Tomás Cruz and persuade him to write this series of books. It's not only an excellent example of the Timba Bomba gear, but also of all the other concepts taught throughout this course. Variations on the Bomba gear can also be heard in the recordings of Bamboleo, Manolín, Issac Delgado, and Charanga Habanera.

Cumbia

Like Merengue and Bomba, the Colombian *Cumbia* began as a folkloric form with its own special drums and has now evolved into a pop music dance genre which is extremely popular throughout the Western Hemisphere and Europe, and which the professional conguero will be expected to be able to perform.

The traditional Cumbia ensemble consisted of two drums: the *alegre* and the *llamador,* plus a bass drum and a maraca-like instrument called the *guache.* Tomasito's adaptation of the rhythm collapses the two drum parts into a marcha playable by one player on two congas. In most popular applications of Cumbia, the low timbal or kick drum is used to cover the bass drum part.

Cumbia has sometimes been used in Cuban Timba, especially by Manolito y su Trabuco, and to a lesser extent by Manolín, el Médico de la Salsa, and Issac Delgado.

Like Bomba, Cumbia has no clave. The DVD chapters use this special click track:

These three Cumbia marchas also serve as excellent technical exercises for developing the abilities of switching between slap and open strokes with the same hand, and slapping with one hand while playing an open stroke with the other.

Marcha 31 – *Cumbia 1* – DVD Chapters 61 & 62

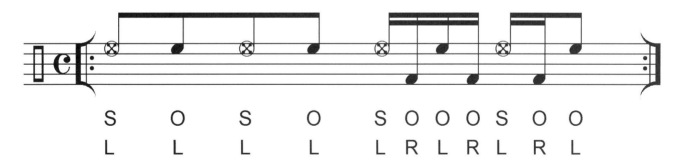

Marcha 32 – *Cumbia 2* – DVD Chapters 63 & 64

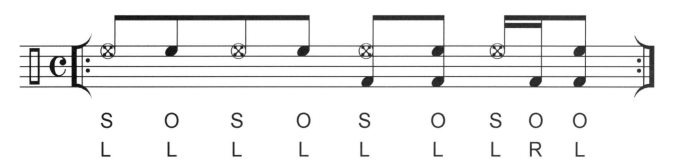

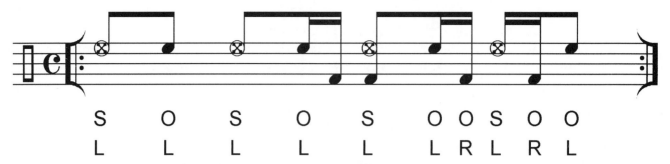

S O S O S O O S O O
L L L L L L R L R L

Cumbia– Recommended Listening

<u>**Folkloric Colombian Cumbia:**</u> (without congas) **"The Rough Guide to Cumbia"** World Music Network (B00004SCES)

<u>**Cumbia adapted to Timba:**</u> **Manolito y su Trabuco** has recorded several arrangements which are nearly pure Cumbia such as *"La Parranda"* from **"Contra todos los prognósticos" (Europtropical EUCD 1).** A more recent Manolito y su Trabuco CD, **"Se rompieron los termómetros" (Eurotropical 8431588907924)**, winner of the 2002 "Cubadisco" award, contains a *"Cumbia Fusión"* arrangement, *"La ciudad"*. One of Tomasito's current Timba bands, **Manolín, el Médico de la Salsa,** lived in Colombia for several months in the mid-90's and the Cumbia influence showed through strongly on several songs, including *"Hay amores"* from **"Para mi gente" (Ahí-Namá 1002-2).** A more subtle example is *"No me mires a los ojos"* from **Issac Delgado: "El año que viene" (RMM 81666).**

PART 7: RECURSOS AND SOLOING

Like any other instrumentalist, the conguero inherits, and hopefully adds to, an arsenal or vocabulary of characteristic "licks" which can be used as fills during exciting sections of songs, or as transitional material between the more spontaneously improvised phrases of solos. In Spanish, these licks are called *recursos*. When playing recursos, the conguero's job is to distinguish himself from the rhythmic orientation of the rest of the rest of the band. This is done with various combinations of syncopation and double, triple, quadruple, sextuple or even octuple time. To further call attention to the congas, recursos are designed to be "noisy", employing the conga's loudest sounds: open tones, open slaps and double strokes with both hands.

Part 8 continues the series of recursos which began in Volume I. Each exercise begins with a normal marcha, transitions into the recurso and then returns to the marcha. As with the marchas, there are two DVD chapters for each recurso, the first at normal speed and the second in slow motion.

Recurso 1 – DVD Chapters 67 & 68

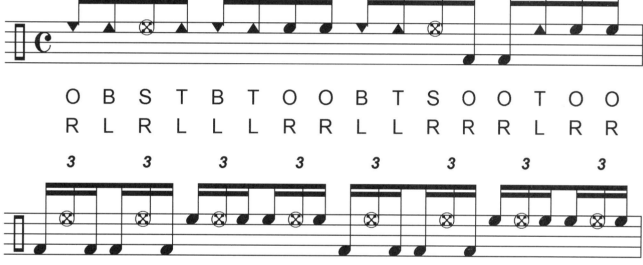

Soloing – Recommended Listening

Here's a short and incomplete list of some of the greatest conga soloists and their recordings:

Tata Güines, one of the first to play two congas, played a seminal role in the development of conga soloing and is listed as an influence by almost everyone who followed him. He incorporated rapid manoteo, flams, rolls, and even a rapid fingernail ruff into the solo vocabulary. One of his many classic solos is *"Descarga Cubana"* from **Israel "Cachao" López: "Descargas: Cuban Jam Sessions" (EGREM 0169).** These historic recordings also feature many other key historical figures including timbalero Guillermo Barreto, and of course, Cachao himself.

Giovanni Hidalgo is arguably the most complete conguero – a child prodigy who fully assimilated all the indigenous genres of his native Puerto Rico as well as every major Cuban innovation. His virtuosity, creativity and stylistic variety and integrity are unparalleled. In the non-instructional performance video **"Giovanni & Changuito – Conga Masters: Duets" (CPP Media 245)** you get a massive, concentrated dose of Giovanni's best playing as he plays with another of the congueros on our "short list" – Tomasito's teacher, **José Luis "Changuito" Quintana.** While better known as a drummer/timbalero, Changuito's incorporation of drum rudiments, his *"mano secreta"*, and his Songo collaborations with El Yulo forever changed the modern Cuban conga vocabulary. Changuito is interviewed by Giovanni (with English subtitles) in the fascinating video **"The Evolution of the Tumbadoras" (DCI 281).**

Another dazzling virtuoso, **Miguel "Angá" Díaz,** has applied Changuito's techniques differently than Giovanni. A great example of his soloing is on *"María Caracóles"* from **Afro-Cuban All Stars: "A todo Cuba le gusta" (Nonesuch 79476).** Angá and Changuito (on timbales) play together on *"Estrellas a las estrellas"* from **Irakere: "¡Afrocubanisimo!" (Bembe 2012).**

Six celebrated Cuban conga legends arrived in the U.S. prior to the Cuban Revolution. **Chano Pozo,** who died tragically in 1948, solos several times on **Dizzy Gillespie: "The Legendary Big Band Concerts" (Vogue 600125). Carlos "Patato" Valdés** meticulously tuned multiple congas to musical pitches, enabling him to add a previously unexplored level of melodicism to his soloing. Patato trades licks with Giovanni Hidalgo and another of the six Cuban pioneers, **Candido Camero,** on **"The Conga Kings" (Chesky 193),** and with **Mongo Santamaría** on **Tito Puente: "In Percussion" (Tico CD 101),** a unique CD consisting entirely of percussion solos, accompanied by only bass. Santamaría's style was laced with phrases and techniques from folkloric music and his recursos and hard-edged tone have influenced generations of congueros. **Francisco Aguabella,** dubbed "the John Coltrane of the congas" by Carlos Santana, has recorded many albums, including his own **"Agua de Cuba" (Cubop CBCD010). Armando Peraza** arrived in NYC in 1949 and has toured and recorded with everyone from George Shearing to Sly and The Family Stone and Santana. Peraza's sense of compositional form and musicality is demonstrated in *"Drume Negrita"* on Shearing's **"On the Sunny Side of the Strip" (GNP 9055).**

One of New York's greatest modern congueros is **Eddie Montalvo.** Our recommended solo is from *"Todos vuelven"* from **Ruben Blades: "Buscando America" (Elektra 9 60352-2).**

APPENDIX 1: MARCHAS NOTATED IN 8TH NOTES

As explained in Part 2, some marchas which are normally notated in 16th notes in Cuba are notated in 8th notes in the United States.

PART 4: AFRO-CUBAN FOLKLORIC MARCHAS

Marcha 1 – *Guaguancó* – DVD Chapters 1 & 2
2-3 Rumba Clave

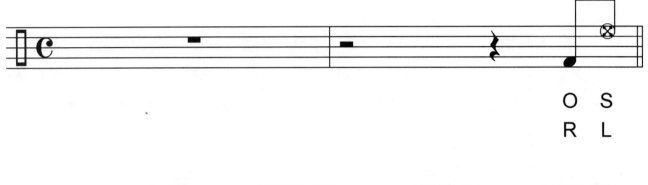

Marcha 2 – *Iyesá* – DVD Chapters 3 & 4
2-3 Rumba Clave

Note: There is no alternative notation for Marchas 3, 4, 5, and 6.

Marcha Changüí – (not included on DVD)

(1st time only)

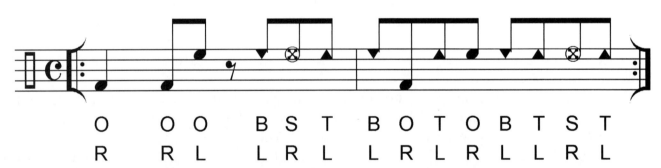

PART 5: MARCHAS FROM OLDER CUBAN POP MUSIC

Special Dengue Click Track

Marcha 7 – *Dengue* – DVD Chapters 13 & 14

```
S  T  B  T  S  T  O  O     O     O  O  S  O
R  L  L  L  R  L  R  L     L     L  R  L  R
```
△
(left hand on drum)

Special Mozambique Click Track

small bell:

campana bell:

toms:

57

Marcha 8 – *Mozambique #1* – DVD Chapters 15 & 16
2-3 Rumba Clave

Marcha 9 – *Mozambique #2* – DVD Chapters 17 & 18
2-3 Rumba Clave

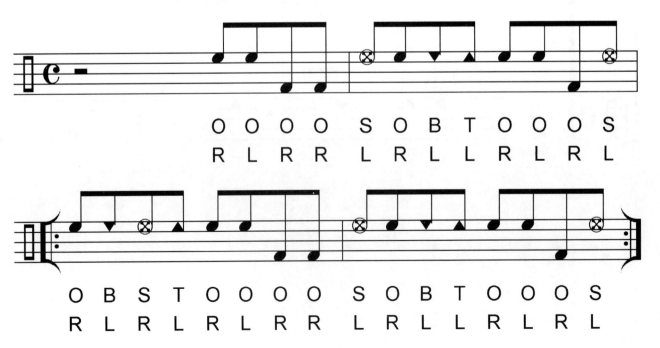

Marcha 10 – *Mozambique #3* – DVD Chapters 19 & 20
2-3 Rumba Clave

Marcha 11 – Original Adaptation of Mozambique – DVD Chapters 21 & 22
2-3 Rumba Clave

B T S T B T O O   B T S O   S O S
L L R L L L R R   L L R R   L R L

O O O   B T S S   B T S O   S O S
R L R   L L R L   R R L R   L R L

O   O   O O S S   B T S O   S O
R   L   R L R L   R R L R   L R

B T S T B T O O   B T S O O S O O
L L R L L L R R   L L R R R L R R

Marcha 12 – *Pilón* – DVD Chapters 23 & 24
3-2 Son Clave

B	O	O	B	S	O	O	O	G
R	R	L	L	R	R	L	R	L	R

B	T	S	T	B	T	B	O	O	B	S	O	O	O	G
L	L	R	L	L	L	R	R	L	L	R	R	L	R	L	R

Marcha 13 – *Suku Suku* – DVD Chapters 25 & 26
2-3 Son Clave

S	T	B	T	S	T	O	T	S	O	B	T	S	T	O	B
R	L	L	L	R	L	R	L	R	L	L	L	R	L	R	L

PART 6: SONGO MARCHAS

Marcha 14 – *Songo básico* – DVD Chapters 27 & 28
2-3 Rumba Clave

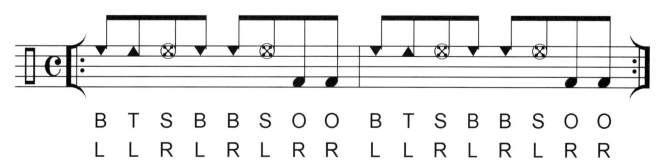

B	T	S	B	B	S	O	O	B	T	S	B	B	S	O	O
L	L	R	L	R	L	R	R	L	L	R	L	R	L	R	R

Marcha 15 – *Songo #2* – DVD Chapters 29 & 30
2-3 Rumba Clave

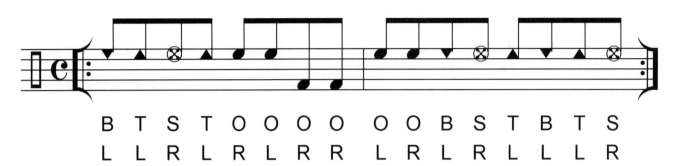

```
B T S T O O O O   O O B S T B T S
L L R L R L R R   L R L R L L L R
```

Marcha 16 – *Songo #3* – DVD Chapters 31 & 32
2-3 Rumba Clave

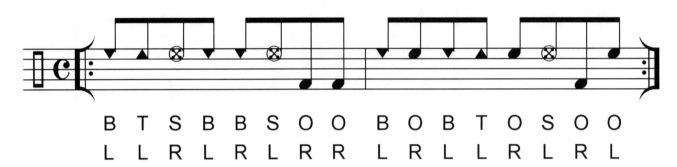

```
B T S B B S O O   B O B T O S O O
L L R L R L R R   L R L L R L R L
```

Songo #3
Alternate Handing 1

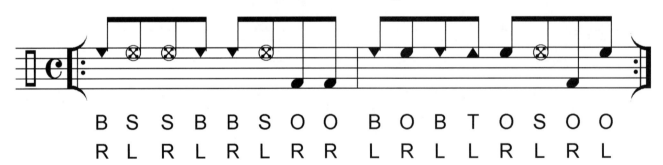

```
B S S B B S O O   B O B T O S O O
R L R L R L R R   L R L L R L R L
```

Songo #3
Alternate Handing 2

```
G B S B B S O O   B O B T O S O O
R L R L R L R R   L R L L R L R L
```

Marcha 17 – *Songo #4* – DVD Chapters 33 & 34
2-3 Rumba Clave

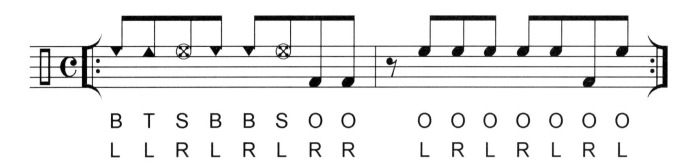

```
B T S B B S O O   O O O O O O
L L R L R L R R   L R L R L R L
```

Marcha 18 – *Songo #5* – DVD Chapters 35 & 36
2-3 Rumba Clave

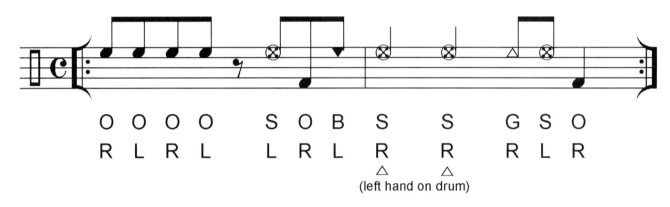

```
O O O O   S O B S   S     G S O
R L R L   L R L R   R     R L R
                △       △
             (left hand on drum)
```

Marcha 19 – *Songo #6* – *Songo con marcha 1* – DVD Chapters 37 & 38
2-3 Rumba Clave

```
                              O O B
                              L R L

S   S O O S   O   B T S G B O O B
R   L R R L   R   L L R R L L R L
```

Marcha 20 – *Songo #7 – Songo con marcha 2* – DVD Chapters 39 & 40
2-3 Rumba Clave

Marcha 21 – *Songo #8* – DVD Chapters 41 & 42
3-2 Rumba Clave

Marcha 22 – *Songo #9* – DVD Chapters 43 &44
2-3 Rumba Clave

Marcha 23 – *Merensongo* – DVD Chapters 45 & 46
3-2 Rumba Clave

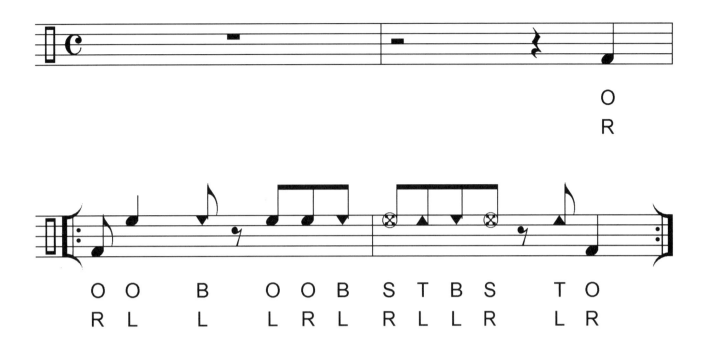

Marcha 24 – *Bota básico* – DVD Chapters 47 & 48
2-3 Rumba Clave

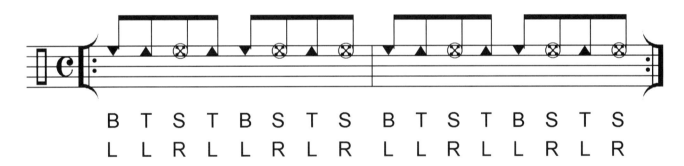

Marcha 25 – *Bota #2* – DVD Chapters 49 & 50
2-3 Rumba Clave

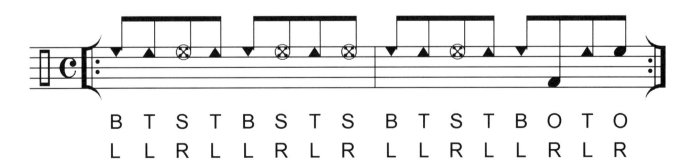

Marcha 26 – *Bota #3* – DVD Chapters 51 & 52
2-3 Rumba Clave

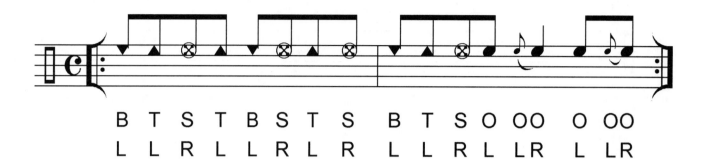

```
B T S T B S T S   B T S O OO  O OO
L L R L L R L R   L L R L LR  L LR
```

Bota #3 – alternate version

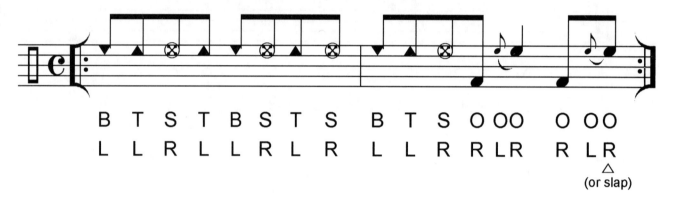

```
B T S T B S T S   B T S O OO  O OO
L L R L L R L R   L L R R LR  R LR
                               △
                            (or slap)
```

PART 7: MARCHAS FROM NON-CUBAN RHYTHMS
Marcha 27 – *Merengue* – DVD Chapters 53 & 54

```
S T B T S T O    O O   B S T O T
R L L L R L R    R L   L R L R L
```

Marcha 28 – *Merengue Apambichao* – DVD Chapters 55 & 56

Marcha 29 – *Bomba 1* – DVD Chapters 57 & 58

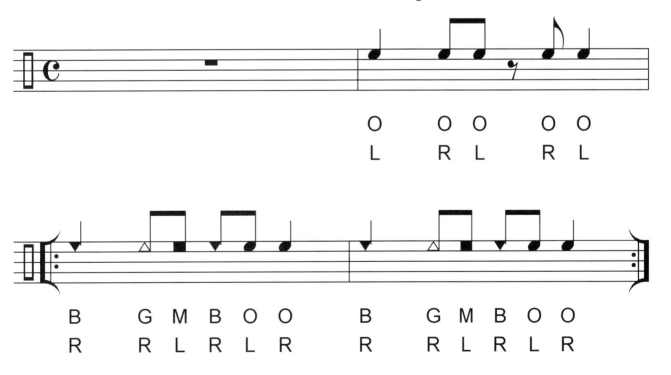

Special Bomba Click Trick

Plena (not on DVD)

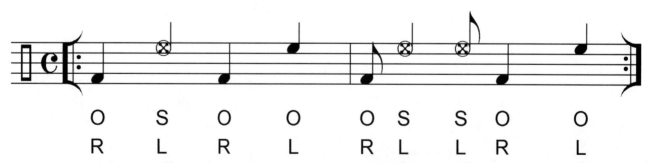

Special Cumbia Click Trick

Marcha 31 – *Cumbia 1* – DVD Chapters 61 & 62

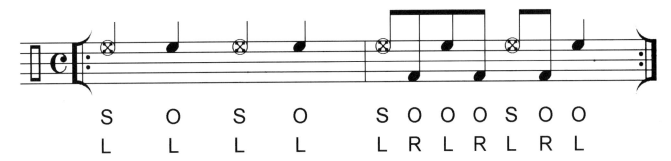

```
S   O   S   O    S O O O S O O
L   L   L   L    L R L R L R L
```

Marcha 32 – *Cumbia 2* – DVD Chapters 63 & 64

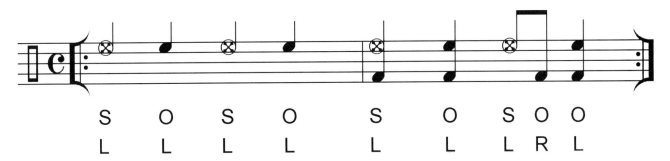

```
S   O   S   O    S   O   S O O
L   L   L   L    L   L   L R L
```

Marcha 33 – *Cumbia 3* – DVD Chapters 65 & 66

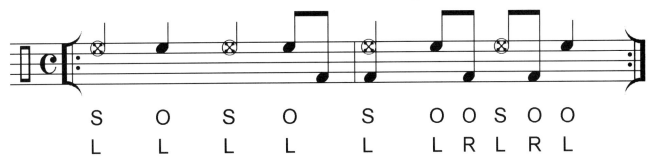

```
S   O   S   O    S   O O S O O
L   L   L   L    L   L R L R L
```

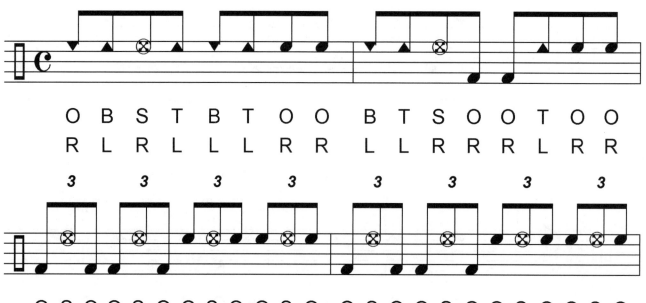

```
O B S T B T O O   B T S O O T O O
R L R L L L R R   L L R R R L R R
```

```
O S O O S O O S O O S O   O S O O S O O S O O S O
R L R R L R L R L L L R L   R L R R L R L R L L L R L
```

```
O B S T B T O O   B T S O O T O O
R L R L L L R R   L L R R R L R R
```

Tomás with El Médico de la Salsa
Photo by Duniel Deya

```
B T S T B T O O   B T S O O T O O
L L R L L L R R   L L R R R L R R
```

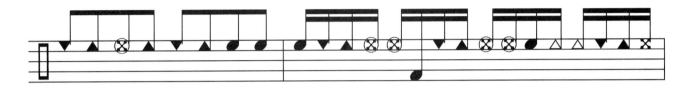

```
B T S T B T O O   O B T S S O B T S S O G G B T os
L L R L L L R R   R L L R L R L L R L R L R L L R
```

```
os B S T B T O O   B T S O O T O O
   L L R L L L R R   L L R R R L R R
```

Photo by Duniel Deya

71

APPENDIX 2: CLAVE

Part 1: Overview

Clave is one of the most important, compelling, and sometimes confusing aspects of studying Latin music. To Cuban musicians like Tomasito, the clave rhythm is as natural as breathing, and like breathing, is something that simply doesn't require intellectual analysis. It's just a fact of life. Clave to a Cuban musician is like the backbeat snare drum is to an American musician. You can play it, vary it, play against it, or leave it out all together, but the feeling of it, like gravity, is always unmistakably and undeniably present.

But to those students of Latin music who are not so lucky as to have been born with "clave in the blood", the term has an altogether different significance. To them, trying to learn to feel and understand the clave is akin to the quest for the Holy Grail. On the one hand, the more you study clave, the easier and more natural playing Latin music becomes, but at the same time, the more you learn, the more you'll realize there *is* to learn about clave.

Part 2 of this section provides you with the essential information about clave that you need to study Volume I while avoiding too much confusing detail. Part 3 goes into greater detail, looking ahead to the challenges of Volumes II & III, and finally, Part 4 deals with some of the apparent contradictions in terminology and notation which have left Latin music students pulling out their collective hair for decades.

Part 2: A Beginner's Introduction to Clave

Clave is a 5-stroke repeating rhythm pattern which is present or implied in most Latin music. There are various types of clave but let's begin with the two we call "2-3 Rumba Clave" and "2-3 Son Clave". In Parts 3 & 4, we'll discuss the widespread disagreement and confusion about the *names* of these rhythms, but for now let's just agree to use these two terms and listen to rhythms.

Listen to the beginning of DVD Chapter 1. The bell comes right on the beat and the other sound is the Jam Block playing 2:3 Rumba Clave. Keep repeating the beginning of this DVD Chapter until you can sing or clap the bell part or the clave while listening to the other.

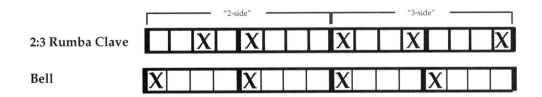

Now listen to the beginning of DVD Chapter 25. The only difference is that the last stroke of the clave comes one subdivision earlier:

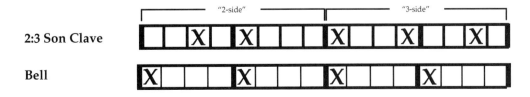

As you read through the rest of this section, remember that a comprehensive understanding of clave is much less important than developing the following two abilities, which are critical:

1) **Be able to clap the clave while you listen to the marcha.**

2) **Be able to play the marcha while someone else plays the clave.**

Part 3: Towards a Deeper Understanding of Clave

To understand the role of clave as a governing principle in rhythm, let's start by separating it from two other governing principles which are independent of the clave: the beat, and the subdivisions of the beat.

The Beat: Put on your favorite recording and tap your foot along with the music. Depending on the song, this tapping might be slower or faster, but the taps, like heartbeats, always come at regular intervals. The speed of these "beats" is called the "tempo". Now put on DVD Chapter 1 and tap your foot along with the bell. The bell is playing the beat. DVD Chapter 2 is a slower performance of the same marcha. In both cases, the bell plays the beat – only the tempo changes. In each case, make sure that you don't find yourself tapping your foot twice as fast as the bell, a common beginner's mistake.

As you listen to and play various types of Latin dance music you'll frequently hear the beat played on this same type of bell, called the *campana*, or *cencerro*, or "bongo bell". It's traditionally hand-held and played by the bongocero, but in modern Cuban music it's sometimes mounted on a stand and played by either the timbalero or the trap drummer. In most cases, the campana pattern, or *campaneo*, is decorated with additional, higher pitched strokes played on the heel of the bell. How these notes are chosen is very definitely determined by the clave, but the steady flow of open bell tones is independent of the clave. The DVD click tracks use just the open bell tones, giving you the beat in its purest form.

The Subdivisions of the Beat: Depending on the style of music, each beat may be subdivided into 2, 3, 4, or more subdivisions. Like the beats themselves, these subdivisions come at regular intervals. For example, rock & roll usually has two subdivisions per beat, while a blues shuffle has three and funk, rap and hip-hop usually have four. The great majority of popular Latin rhythms have four subdivisions per beat, although Afro-Cuban folkloric rhythms (see Volume II), can have three or four subdivisions and in some cases both simultaneously! Also, like hip-hop and jazz, some of these folkloric rhythms place certain strokes *between* the 1/3 and 1/4 subdivisions, creating an effect sometimes called "swing".

Keeping this idea of subdivisions in mind, listen again to DVD Chapter 1 and notice that the conga marcha consists of exactly four evenly-spaced strokes for each beat of the campana bell. To hear this in slow motion, listen to DVD Chapter 2. Now scan through some of the other marchas you've studied, noting that in every case, the conga marcha consists of all four subdivisions of each beat, with none left out and nothing else added. The conga is the only instrument in the popular Latin ensemble which consistently plays all the subdivisions (except of course during solos).

To summarize, the principal job of the bell player is to state the beat and yours, as the conguero, is to state the subdivisions of the beat. Both of these functions are independent of the clave.

Listen once again to DVD Chapters 1 & 2, being conscious of the bell playing the beat and the conga playing the subdivisions. What's left is the clave itself.

The Clave: The clave pattern consists of 5 strokes asymmetrically arranged across 4 beats, or across a total of 16 subdivisions. Leaving aside the folkloric rhythms studied in Part 3 that use three subdivisions per beat, there are four clave patterns that the conguero will encounter:

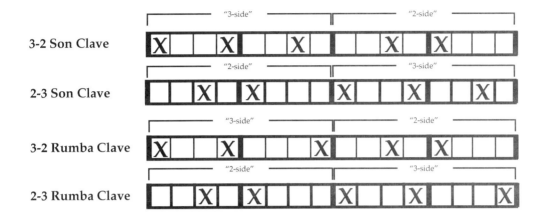

Note that the terms "3-side" and "2-side" are derived from the amount of strokes in each 2-beat section and that the "3-2" and "2-3" versions of each clave are really the same rhythm starting on a different "side". We'll explain some of the confusion about these two subjects in Part 4.

Clave and the Instruments of the Latin Ensemble: The rhythm patterns of each instrument in the Latin ensemble are influenced by the clave. It's very important for the conguero to know the parts of the other percussionists and how they relate to the clave.

The clave rhythm itself can be played with two sticks (themselves called claves), but is more often played by the timbalero or trap drummer on a plastic woodblock-like instrument known as a "jam block". Sometimes the clave rhythm is not played at all, but the musicians and informed listeners can still hear where the 2-side and 3-side are by listening to the parts of the other instruments, which imply the clave just as strongly.

The following examples are shown starting on the 2-side of the clave. 2-3 Rumba Clave is shown as a reference, but the patterns would be the same when played against 2-3 Son Clave. The key point is that the 2-side of the pattern must stay in sync with the 2-side of the clave.

Campaneo: The campana, or cencerro bell states the beat with open tones ("O") and marks the clave with the heel ("H") of the bell. An accented single "H", on the 2-side imitates the clave.

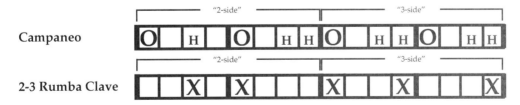

Contracampaneo: The *contracampana*, or "mambo bell", or "timbale bell" pattern is played on a smaller mounted bell by either the timbalero or trap drummer. It also clearly accents the 2-side and has a characteristically more-syncopated rhythm on the 3-side.

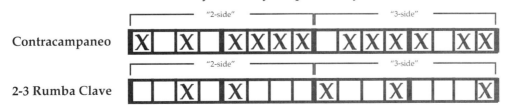

Cáscara: The *cáscara* rhythm is played on the side, or shell, of the higher timbale drum, and also sometimes on the ride cymbal.

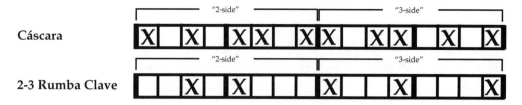

The parts of the piano, bass, horns, voices, kick drum and congas vary greatly from style to style and from arrangement to arrangement, but they, like everything in Latin music, are always affected by the presence of the clave. There are even cases, especially with the kick drum and more complex conga marchas, where an instrument intentionally plays *"contraclave"*, or "against the clave". Such an example is the *Guaguancó* rhythm where the open conga tones outline the 3-side against the 2-side of the clave. The "gravitational force" of the clave is always present, but how creative arrangers and musicians deal with that force leaves a lot of room for artistic discretion.

Clave and Conga Marchas:

Now let's take a look at the relationship between the clave and some of the marchas we've already studied. For these examples, we'll show only the first letter of the name of each stroke, using a lower-case "o" for the open stroke on the smaller "quinto" (or *macho*) drum and an upper-case "O" for the open stroke on the larger "tumba" (or *hembra)* drum.

First let's review Marchas 1, 2, 3, and 5 from Volume I:

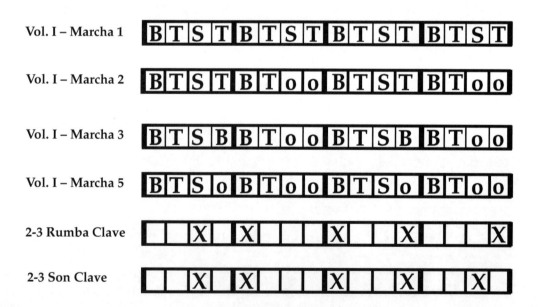

Note that in Marchas 2, 3, and 5 the pattern repeats after 8 strokes, and in Marcha 1, it repeats after only 4. It follows that you wind up playing exactly the same sequence of strokes on the 2-side as you do against the 3-side. These marchas are perfect for use in under-rehearsed gigs and jam sessions when you don't know in advance what the clave is. You can play these "safe marchas" until the direction of the clave becomes clear and then switch to something more adventurous.

Now let's look at Marchas 4 & 6 of Volume I:

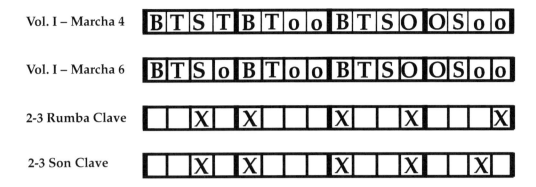

These marchas, like the clave itself, continue for 16 subdivisions before repeating, and are traditionally played so that the two open tumba tones are played on the 3 side. This is called "playing the big drum on the 3-side", an interesting convention discussed further in Part 4. When playing an arrangement that's "in 3-2" (also see Part 4), you would invert these marchas like this:

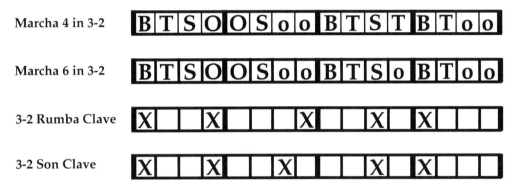

The relationship between clave and marcha is of paramount importance, so study the two diagrams above until you're certain you completely understand them! If you have any doubts, feel free to email us at **kevin@timba.com**. We'll be happy to clarify anything that doesn't make sense.

Part 4: Clave Confusion Stemming from Terminology and Notation

Even the best percussionists can often be heard arguing endlessly about the terms and concepts surrounding the elusive subject of clave. It's a great understatement to say that "clave is something that should be felt, and not talked about!" But clave's "Catch-22" is that unless you were born hearing it, you have to go through a sometimes painful period of trying to understand it well enough to teach yourself to feel it and there are some nasty roadblocks standing in the way of those trying to understand it!

Here are some of the most common:

1) 8th notes versus 16th notes

2) "3-2 clave" versus "2-3 clave"

3) "Son Clave" versus "Rumba Clave"

4) "Playing the big drum on the 3-side"

5) "Clave Changes" and "Jumping the Clave"

Let's tackle them one by one:

8th notes versus 16th notes

In Cuba, music is usually written in 16th notes such that one clave lasts one measure, but outside of Cuba, music is usually written in 8th notes such that one clave lasts two measures. Most instructional books on the market also use the 8th note method. We include both.

Here are 3 ways of writing the same rhythm, 3-2 Rumba Clave:

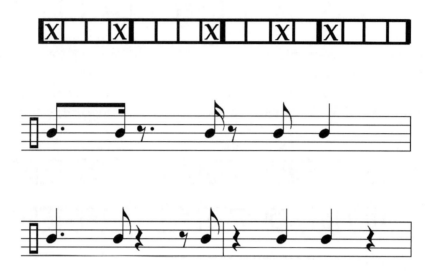

The "box" diagram at the top is the least ambiguous, showing the 4 main beats, each with 4 subdivisions, for a total of 16 possible locations, of which the clave occupies 5. Of the other two notation examples, the 16th note method really makes more sense because it shows the rhythm over the space of 4 quarter notes, and, in common time, or 4/4, a quarter note gets one beat. If you were to take the 8th note diagram literally, you would conclude that one clave lasts 8 beats, each with 2 subdivisions, which, as we pointed out above, is completely wrong and will result in a beginner feeling the clave incorrectly. Nevertheless, unless you live in Cuba, almost all the written Latin music you encounter will be written in 8th notes and you will simply be expected to know that you have to "think in 2/2", or "cut time" so that you're still only feeling 4 beats per clave. The advantage of this method is that the page looks less cluttered and many professional musicians find it much easier to read. Your eye doesn't have to decipher the double-flagged sixteenth notes and sixteenth rests, or the dotted rests.

To please everyone, we supply both types of notation, with the 8th note versions in a special appendix. In a close call, we chose the 16th note method for the main text to be sure that beginners understand that a clave lasts 4 beats, not 8.

Of course, many of the best professional congueros don't even know how to read music and play by ear. As we pointed out in the introduction, if you yourself don't know how to read music, you've probably discovered that it's very easy to "read" the exercises in this book by simply looking at the letters beneath the notes.

Note: The earliest examples of notation in Cuba were written in 16th notes, but in a 2/4 time signature, such that the clave lasted 2 bars, but the beat was still accurately represented.

"3-2 clave" versus "2-3 clave"

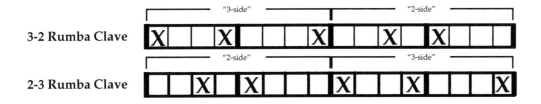

These are really the same rhythm, starting in different places. The only difference is where you start counting "1, 2, 3, 4", or, in 16th note notation, where the barlines are.

If you walked into a room where someone had already begun playing clave, you wouldn't be able to say whether it was "3-2" or "2-3" because the clave rhythm is a repeating loop and you wouldn't know where the person had started, or where the person was imagining the barlines to be. However, if the piano, bass, voices and horns were to come in and make it clear where the barlines were, you could then say that musical piece was "in 2-3" or "in 3-2".

Or could you? Most of the time, it's quite obvious where the barlines are when you hear the whole band playing together, but sometimes, because of the nature of pickups, it's actually possible that even *with* the whole band playing, two listeners could perceive the barlines as being in different places. Furthermore, some Cuban music has intentionally ambiguous over-lapping phrases such that one instrument might seem to be putting its "barlines" on one side of the clave while another puts them on the other side! If this seems far-fetched, try this experiment: get a group of musicians or Latin music fans together to listen to recordings, asking each person to show where he or she hears the "1, 2, 3, 4", especially during the "coro" sections that are found in the second halves of the arrangements. Some interesting choices might be "*¿Y ahora qué?*" by Paulito FG, "*Extraños ateos*" by David Calzado y La Charanga Habanera, and "*Güiro, calabaza, y miel*" by Manolito y su Trabuco. You may be surprised to discover that often a section which sounds like it's obviously in 3-2 to you will sound like it's in 2-3 to someone else.

The only way to be 100% sure whether you're in 3-2 or 2-3 is to actually look at the written chart and see where the barlines are written and even this would only work if the chart were written in 16th notes, because in 8th notes there's a separate bar for each "side" of the clave. This is another argument in favor of writing music in 16th notes. Since each clave takes only one measure, the arranger is forced to reveal how he or she hears the "1, 2, 3, 4".

But some bands, such as Bamboleo, don't even use charts – even the horn players learn their parts by ear in rehearsal. Because the only difference between "2-3" and "3-2" is where one subjectively hears the barlines, it's even theoretically possible for two musicians in the same band to have their clave-based parts in sync while each perceives the musical phrases of the arrangement as beginning on different sides! And as we pointed out earlier, sometime arrangers intentionally set the instruments off against each other for artistic reasons. In short, written music with its time signatures and barlines is sometimes simply not adequate to represent the complex rhythms of some Cuban music and while the concept of "2-3 and 3-2" is very practical and useful in most cases, it has also has inherent potential for causing mass confusion.

So what's a poor conguero to do? Not to worry. It doesn't matter where you subjectively per-ceive the "1, 2, 3, 4" as long as the 2-side of your marcha lines up with the 2-side of the clave and the 3-side of your marcha lines up with the 3-side of the clave. As in, for example, Marchas

14 & 24 of this book, the marcha pattern is the same on both sides of the clave, so you couldn't get it wrong if you tried, but if you're using a marcha which is different on each side of the clave (e.g. Marcha 15 or 26), you have to be able to hear where the clave is and make your part line up with it. Fortunately, when in doubt, you can always just play a clave-neutral marcha until you figure out where the clave is.

Son Clave versus Rumba Clave

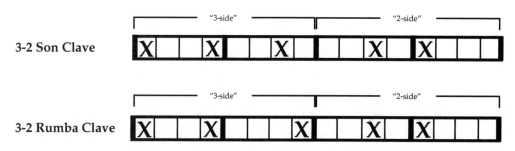

As we've already discussed, the only difference between Son and Rumba Clave is that the third stroke of the 3-side comes one subdivision later in Rumba Clave, creating a more syncopated rhythm. Some genres (e.g. *Guaguancó*) and some groups (e.g. La Charanga Habanera) use Rumba Clave exclusively while others use Son Clave exclusively. Still others (e.g. Issac Delgado, Los Van Van, Klimax) switch from section to section and many groups will in fact alternate back and forth between Son & Rumba Clave almost randomly within the same section. To hear such an example, listen to the legendary studio recording of NG La Banda's "Santa Palabra". Even the more traditional group Orquesta Aragón sometimes switches between Son & Rumba Clave in the middle of the same coro section. So while a *Guaguancó* should always use Rumba Clave and a *Chachachá* should always use Son Clave, there are also many cases where either or both can be used, so it's necessary to avoid being too rigid about the distinction between these two rhythms.

For example, in Volume I, note that the DVD click tracks for Marchas 5 & 6 use Son Clave, while Marchas 1-4 use Rumba Clave. It's very unlikely that Chachachá marchas like Marchas 5 & 6 would ever use Rumba Clave, but any of Marchas 1-4 could just as easily be played with Son Clave.

Thus, as a conguero, what you need to know is where the 2-side and 3-side are, regardless of whether it's Son or Rumba Clave, and to know which side of your marcha (if it has 2 different sides) goes with which side of the clave.

The names of the different types of clave rhythms are also the source of frequent confusion. What we call "Son Clave" is this book is sometimes called "Puerto Rican Clave", and what we call "Rumba Clave" is sometimes called "Cuban Clave" or *"Clave de Guaguancó"*. We've heard the term *"Clave Cubana"* used for both types. The naming confusion even extends to the numbers. The rhythm we call "3-2 Rumba Clave":

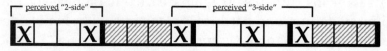

...is sometimes called "2-3" by those who don't read music, because of the distance between the notes as opposed to their placement relative to the beats. For more on this often humorous debate, and more on clave in general, we refer you to the internet articles published at: http://clave.timba.com.

"Playing the big drum on the 3-side"

This is another area where trying to be too rigid will get you into nothing but trouble! Let's look again at the way that Marcha 4 from Volume I, lines up with the clave:

Tomás presents this marcha so that the low tones occur on the 3-side. This is often referred to as "playing the big drum on the 3-side" and in many Latin playing situations, it's considered very wrong to do it the other way and play this figure on the 2-side. However, take this with a grain of salt because when you get to the Timba marchas in Volume III you'll find many examples where these same two low drum tones occur on the 2-side.

"Clave Changes" and "Jumping the Clave"

As we pointed out above, the flow of the melody and harmony cause the listener to perceive the phrases of the music as beginning on the 2-side ("2-3 Clave") or the 3-side ("3-2 Clave"). A good arranger will write musical phrases which flow naturally with the clave, but what if one section sounds better starting on the 3-side and another on the 2-side? One solution is to devise a transitional phrase which is a half a clave longer or shorter than normal. For example:

Phrase 1: 2-3-2-3-2-3-2-3 etc.
Transitional Phrase: 2-3-2
Phrase 2: 3-2-3-2-3-2-3-2 etc.

In this example, the alternating flow of the clave is uninterrupted but the perceived clave changes from 2-3 to 3-2. Of course, as we pointed out above, the perceived beginning of the phrase is in the ear of the beholder, so the arranger's skill and creativity, or lack thereof, can intentionally or unintentionally result in varying percentages of listeners perceiving a clave change. A skillful arranger, if desired, can make the change so obvious that virtually all listeners perceive the clave change in the same place, but the same skillful arranger may prefer to leave the "plot" open to multiple interpretations. It's all a matter of artistic choice.

The arranger can also "jump the clave" by intentionally constructing the chart so that the percussionists are required to play the 2-side or the 3-side twice in a row. While easier for dancers, this is significantly harder for the musicians because everyone has to agree in advance, at rehearsal, to "jump the clave" at the same place. It's no longer a question of perception, but a matter of cold hard facts. You have to alter the natural flow of the clave and you have to do it at a prescribed moment in time.

For some reason, a particularly high percentage of the greatest masterpieces of all Latin music are heavily-laden with clave changes. Brilliant examples of the first type of clave change can be found in *"Todos vuelven"* by Rubén Blades, and *"Bamboleo"* by the Fania All-Stars. For equally brilliant examples of "jumping the clave", listen to *"No me mires a los ojos"* by Issac Delgado, *"Por encima del nivel"* by Los Van Van, or *"Extraños ateos"* by David Calzado y La Charanga Habanera.

The subject of clave changes is further explored at http://clave.timba.com. For further study of clave and Latin music in general, look for David Peñalosa's upcoming 7-volume series.

APPENDIX 3: BOTA AND SONGO CON EFECTOS

There are no commercially available recordings of the live performances of the Paulito FG band of 1998, so we provide this appendix as a special bonus for readers who are true Timba fanatics willing to go to greater lengths to pursue this esoteric but rewarding subject. We suggest studying it only after completing Volume III of this series.

Overview

In the live performance style of 1998 Paulito FG group, each song in a live performance lasts between ten and twenty minutes. A typical performance begins with an extended introduction, borrowing coros from later in the arrangement, followed by a fairly faithful recreation of the material on the studio recording. After this comes an open-ended series of coros, horn mambos, solos, guest appearances and breakdowns, including extensive audience participation and often involving the invention of new coros based on the events of the evening in question. During each of these individual sections, the band can "shift gears" one or more times, cued by hand signals given by the singer or musical director. The key concept to understand is that the changes in the "gear" of the rhythm section often do *not* coincide with the changes between the sections of the overall arrangement. For example, the rhythm section could go into the *Songo con efectos* or *Bomba* gear while the singers continue their call and response, or *coro/guía* section, as if nothing has changed.

Structure

The Songo con Efectos section always begins with a flourish, or "ruff" played by both the congas and drums. Regardless of the clave, the ruff always ends on the downbeat of the first measure of the Songo con Efectos section. The ruff can be played with slaps or opens.

At this point, the bass drops out, the drummer breaks down to clave and kick drum, and the bongocero, who has been playing steady time on the campana bell, stops his pattern and begins to play sparsely and freely. The piano, voices and horns continue with no change to their parts other than an intensification of certain accents. The conguero begins to play a variant of the Bota and the other two percussionists respond improvisationally. The next key element to be described is the addition of the "efectos". For each individual song the arrangers of the Paulito band created one or more specific, very sparse bass parts which we'll call "songo riffs".

Other than playing these short pre-determined riffs, the bass is completely silent, drawing the listeners' attention to the percussion section, which in turn dramatizes the bass part by playing *bloques* (rhythmic punches) to accent and/or complement it. These percussion bloques are also played the same way each time. All the percussion between the bloques is improvised, using Bota as a starting reference point. Towards the end of 1998, the Paulito group was using up to six or seven Songo con Efectos sections per song and the improvisations became freer and freer, creating the exhilirating effect of all three percussionists soloing simultaneously while the horns and singers continued their normal parts.

Here are two examples of Bota variations which can be used as a basis for improvisation between the bloques:

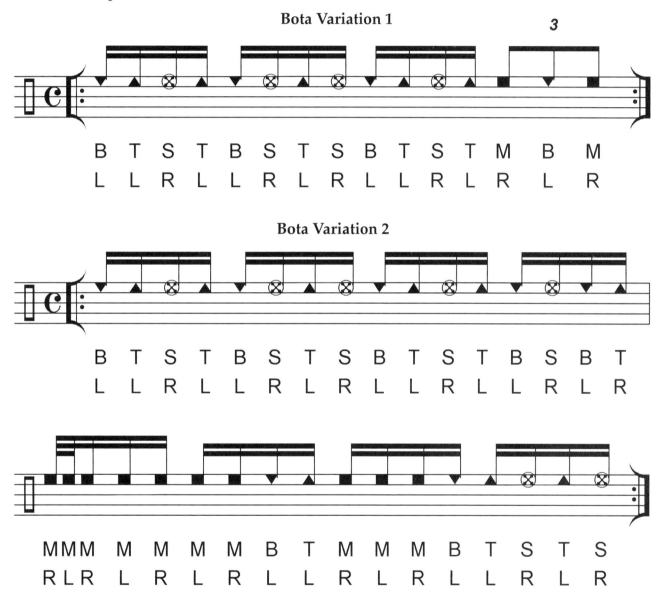

On the following pages are several "textbook" examples of how Tomasito would negotiate the main elements of a Songo con Efectos section, staying fairly close to the basic Bota rhythm. All are from live versions of songs from the Paulito FG album "Con la Conciencia Tranquila", except the last, on page 88, which is from a song originally performed by the 1998 Paulito group called *"La última bala"*. It was finally recorded in 2000, as *"Una vez más"*, by a different rhythm section, on the album *"Una vez más...por amor"*. The bloque was the same, but the conga marcha was different, with less of an emphasis on Bota. The transcription shows the way Tomasito played it.

Songo con Efectos Section of *"Llamada anónima"*
3-2 Rumba Clave

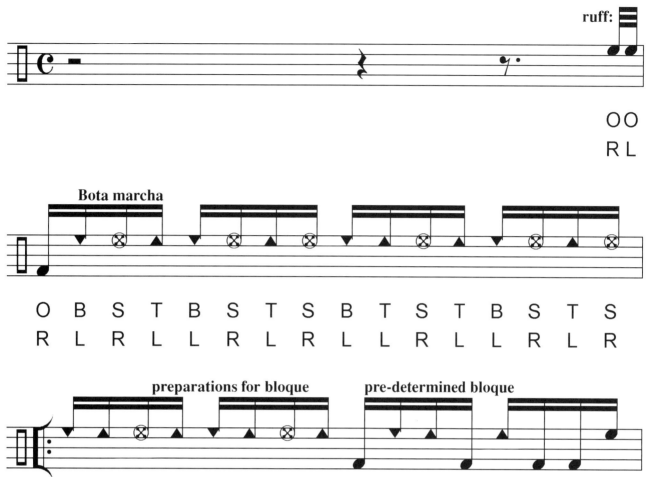

While many Timba bands have recorded examples of the Bomba gear, Songo con efectos was unique to the Paulito group and after adding it the group didn't record again until after Tomasito and other key members of the rhythm section such as drummer Yoel Páez and bassist Joel Domínguez had left. There are several examples of a gear similar to Songo con Efectos on the 2000 release, **Paulo FG: "Una vez más...por amor" (Promusic CDP-0013).** One comes at 4:38 of *"Una vez más"*, (called *"La última bala"* when it was played by the earlier group), and a second example comes at 4:42 of *"Enredadera de amor"*. Ironically, while these sections follow the basic structure of Songo con Efectos, the conguero doesn't refer to the *Bota* rhythm, so it's "Songo con Efectos" without the Songo! This is another reason why we chose to relegate this section to the Appendix to be discovered only by those with the temerity and patience to sort out the many confusing details. We suggest studying this section *after* completing Volume III of this course.